'In an age when whining has bec...... a pandemic, when entitlement sits cheek by jowl with incessant dubious claims of victimization, Peter Maiden provides us with an alternative – a profoundly biblical alternative. In twelve short chapters, he not only exhorts his readers to thankfulness but also fleshes out a plethora of reasons to be grateful. He also paints pictures of the glory of gratitude – a gospel duty and privilege, and a mark of faith.'

D. A. Carson, Emeritus Professor of New Testament at Trinity Evangelical Divinity School, Deerfield, Illinois, Founder/President of the Gospel Coalition and author of more than fifty books, including *How Long, O Lord? Reflections on suffering and evil* and *A Call to Spiritual Reformation: Priorities from Paul and his prayers*

'I was thrilled when Peter agreed to write this book for Keswick Ministries, and my expectations have not been disappointed. *Radical Gratitude* is inspiring; it is made all the more poignant and powerful by Peter's recent diagnosis. It will help you to discover the power of gratitude to transform your outlook and energize your service. Even better, it will point you to the true fuel of gratitude – the amazing grace of God.'

Tim Chester, Chair of Keswick Ministries, Pastor of Grace Church, Boroughbridge, faculty member of Crosslands Training and author of forty books, including *You Can Change: God's transforming power for our sinful behaviour and negative emotions*

'With profound sincerity and simplicity, this inspirational book teaches us the vital importance of a grateful heart, replacing the proud self-sufficiency and grumbling anxiety of

our age. And so we discover the secret of quiet trust and joyful contentment. Through moving personal testimony and lively biblical examples, Peter points us to a way of life that rejoices in God's fatherly care, trusts his sovereign control and, daily, enjoys his gracious provision. A hugely refreshing, encouraging and life-changing read!'
Jonathan Lamb, Minister-at-Large, Keswick Ministries, and author of *Essentially One: Striving for the unity God loves*

'Gratitude is a choice – we cannot control our circumstances, but we can control our responses. Through personal testimony and a faithful engagement with Scripture, Peter Maiden helps us to cultivate a deep-seated delight in God's grace, which leads to a heart overflowing with gratitude. Amid all the vagaries of life, we can still affirm that it is well with our souls. The book is inspiring and moving, as well as being radically countercultural. Read it and be blessed.'
Paul Mallard, Senior Minister, Widcombe Baptist Church, Bath, former President of the Fellowship of Independent Evangelical Churches and author of *Invest Your Suffering: Unexpected intimacy with a loving God*, *Invest Your Disappointments: Going for growth*, *Staying Fresh: Serving with joy* and *An Identity to Die For: Know who you are*

'This is a wonderful, inspiring book! It addresses a topic that we desperately need in our anxious age of entitlement: gratitude is the hallmark of the Christian life because it helps us to understand that God's grace is an extravagant, undeserved gift from our loving God. Peter Maiden excels in showing us how to develop contentment and gratitude while still being honest about our struggles and weaknesses. His wisdom,

experience and biblical insight flows through every page. Read it and share it!'
Rebecca Manley Pippert, author of *Stay Salt: The world has changed – our message must not*

'Drawing from deep personal experiences and biblical truths, Peter shares his life and ministry journey, which have shaped him to be who he is today! *Radical Gratitude* is a timely reminder of the need for a thankful heart in all circumstances. It is intimate, challenging and inspiring – an authentic reflection of the author, his faith and his service to our sovereign God.'
Lawrence Tong, International Director, Operation Mobilisation

'I pray that this book will lead to a practical, measurable revolution of thankfulness.'
George Verwer, founder of Operation Mobilisation, author and speaker

RADICAL GRATITUDE

RADICAL GRATITUDE

Recalibrating your heart in an
age of entitlement

Peter Maiden

INTER-VARSITY PRESS
36 Causton Street, London SW1P 4ST, England
Email: ivp@ivpbooks.com
Website: www.ivpbooks.com

First published in 2020

British Library Cataloguing-in-Publication Data
A catalogue record for this book is available from the British Library.

ISBN: 978-1-78974-185-8
eBook ISBN: 978-1-78974-186-5

10 9 8 7 6 5 4 3 2 1

Set in 11.75/15.5pt Minion Pro
Typeset in Great Britain by CRB Associates, Potterhanworth, Lincolnshire
Printed in Great Britain by Ashford Colour Press

Inter-Varsity Press publishes Christian books that are true to the Bible and that communicate the gospel, develop discipleship and strengthen the church for its mission in the world.

IVP originated within the Inter-Varsity Fellowship, now the Universities and Colleges Christian Fellowship, a student movement connecting Christian Unions in universities and colleges throughout Great Britain, and a member movement of the International Fellowship of Evangelical Students. Website: www.uccf.org.uk. That historic association is maintained, and all senior IVP staff and committee members subscribe to the UCCF Basis of Faith.

To my friends and colleagues at Operation Mobilisation
and Keswick Ministries.
I have been so grateful for the privilege of serving
alongside you.

Contents

Foreword

I have just read the manuscript of this book and, to be honest, feel quite humbled to have been asked to write this foreword.

How do I respond to such a powerful, biblical message by one of the people I respect most in God's work? Well, I need to repent, especially for the unkind and ungracious words that have come out of my mouth. I am greatly helped by 1 John 2:1: 'My dear children, I write this to you so that you will not sin. But if anybody does sin, we have an advocate with the Father – Jesus Christ, the Righteous One.' I am only in this race with Peter because of God's forgiveness and transforming grace.

I believe that this book fits well with Peter's other books – *Take My Plastic, Discipleship Matters* and *Building on the Rock* – and would urge you to read them too.

What should be some of the practical outcomes of this book?

1 We need to be filled continually by the Holy Spirit on a daily basis. What Peter has written ties in with Galatians 5:22–23: 'But the fruit of the Spirit is love, joy, peace, forbearance, kindness, goodness, faithfulness, gentleness and self-control.' This great reality will not make a Spirit-filled life automatic though, which takes me to my next point.
2 We need to be more wholehearted in daily following Jesus: 'Whoever wants to be my disciple must deny themselves and take up their cross daily and follow me'

(Luke 9:23). Without this kind of discipline and action, this book will just provide one more head trip. Remember James' exhortation to be 'doers' of the Word, not just 'hearers' (see James 1:22).

3 We must take practical steps to be more gracious. I was asked to speak at the funeral of a dear woman of God. There, I met someone who knew her and her late husband and had spent time in their home. This person was amazed at the gracious words they continually spoke to each other and to others. Bang – I had to repent even before I got up to speak! I have always been filled with gratitude for Drena, my wife; soon we will have been married for sixty years but, because of my temperament and the pressure of work, some unkind, ungracious words have come out of my big New Jersey mouth. No wonder I have always felt that Peter Maiden was more of an angel by comparison with me. I once wrote him a very harsh letter and I well remember his gracious reaction to it. No wonder my favourite short prayer is 'Lord, have mercy on me', and I am glad that one of Peter's themes in this book is mercy.

4 We should be more thankful. I have made it a priority in my life to thank every person for anything they have done for Drena and me or for the work we have been called to. I have done a global survey on this and discovered that most people do not thank others for small gifts or favours, except for saying 'thank you' on the spot when something is handed to them. I pray that this book will lead to a practical, measurable revolution of thankfulness. Yes, it means more notes, cards, emails, phone calls or even a thank-you visit.

5 I hope that reading this book will lead you to be more
   positive, even about negative, messy situations (my book
   Messiology might be of help on this subject[1]). My plea is
   for grace-awakened big-heartedness. Reading this book
   will help you on to that 1 Corinthians 13 path. I hope
   you will buy extra copies and give them away.

In closing, I want to say that one of the huge encouragements
in my life has been meeting and knowing people who, in
Christ, powerfully model the gratitude that Peter writes about.
He, his wife Win and their family are among them. While
writing this foreword, I talked to just such another person on
the phone. I started to make a list of grateful people but there
is not enough space to put it here and, anyway, those on the
list and still alive would not be happy about it. I would hope
that I could be on my list too, but I have my doubts.

George Verwer
Founder, Operation Mobilisation

Introduction
Thirty-six hours

'How's Tim?' would be my anxious, recurring question to my wife Win in those calls from overseas. The first signs of my son's Crohn's disease (an inflammatory bowel disease with no known cause and no known cure) had appeared in his mid teens. Although our son enjoyed periods when the discomfort and pain eased, the respites were short-lived.

In the early days of his struggles, I was the International Director of Operation Mobilisation (OM), a global missionary organization that demanded considerable travel and many weeks at a time away from home.[1] But I would always try to phone home each day, however briefly. Frequently, the news would leave me crying out to God, 'Please give Tim grace to endure this and help Win to bear the brunt while I'm away.' I felt helpless.

Then the nagging questions would start: 'Is this *really* the right job for me? Really? Particularly with Tim's illness being so unpredictable and severe?' For instance, on one occasion, I had been preparing for OM's General Council, the major gathering of our far-flung missionaries in one venue every three or four years. Not only had I spent months sorting out the agenda and papers but I had also spent weeks on the message from Scripture that I was convinced God wanted me to share with our missionaries. My plans were well advanced, we had purchased our travel tickets and everything seemed to be developing nicely. Then the news that I was secretly dreading hit like a bombshell: Tim was seriously ill.

Immediately, I knew where I needed to be: at home with my son. Things deteriorated and Tim's first operation became urgent. The day approached and my emotions became more churned up. The afternoon before the operation I went for a run. It was my usual route of around six miles; I ran it faster than ever before. Perhaps I was motivated by a cocktail of feelings: anger and worry were very much in the mix. How can I describe the relief when I heard that the operation had gone well? When Win and I visited Tim, we saw him not only alive but also apparently enjoying every moment of the 'high' from his pain medication!

But our elation was short-lived. Tim began to feel ill and had to take an anti-sickness drug. We didn't know this at the time but it was, ironically, this drug that provoked the most violent reaction in his body. There followed about thirty-six hours of uncertainty and fear for us all, and fresh agony for my son. He struggled to breathe; he was biting his tongue and his body was writhing out of control. A variety of consultants appeared but none could identify the problem. Sitting beside him, I desperately encouraged him to breathe. I cried out to God to intervene. At one point, my brother arrived with oil to pray for Tim's healing, as prescribed in the New Testament in the epistle of James.

As the hours passed, I was shocked by something else that was disturbing in a different way. There seemed to be no improvement. Indeed, the symptoms seemed only to be getting worse and I was beginning to think the unthinkable: 'These might be my last few hours with my son. God, you can't allow this,' I protested. 'I am your servant and I have sacrificed for you. You owe me . . . You just can't let this happen!'

> *'You owe me . . . You just can't let*
> *this happen!'*

Confidently, I had preached in my sermons, 'God is sovereign and good; you can entrust your life, your family, your future into his hands.' Now, admittedly, I thought I really believed this but, when the rubber hit the road, there I was wanting my own way, unwilling to bow to the sovereign God. Yes, I was absolutely right – and it was quite normal – to cry out to him for healing and intervention, but I wasn't giving him any options, just insisting that *he* did things *my* way. I knew best and there was only one outcome I would be prepared to thank him for.

After those thirty-six hours, a young consultant came into the room. 'I've seen this before,' he commented and proceeded to give Tim an injection. Normality returned; there was relief and gratitude all round – we breathed easily again. As I write this, I am deeply conscious that there might be readers who have suffered similar traumas but without the result I have described. I pray sincerely that there might be comfort in what follows in this book for you.

As I later reflected on those thirty-six hours, I realized with shock and sadness that an entitled way of thinking – something which I had often warned about in my preaching – had ruled supreme in that small room: 'I have done this for you. I expect a response, a return on my investment!' Entitlement thinking, as I will call it in this book, didn't just rule in that room. During my travels over the past forty-five years, I have regularly stayed in places where you cannot turn on a tap and be guaranteed water that is safe to drink. Yet, back at home, I am likely to take clean, harmless water completely for granted. I live in a developed nation and, if I am paying my taxes, then, surely, I'm entitled to enjoy such things as safe drinking water, aren't I? And I'm not alone. Recently, a missionary to an African nation, experiencing some of the daily frustrations of life, wrote to a Westerner, 'I have realized that entitlement has been the root of my difficulties in giving thanks in all circumstances.'[2]

Never again would I want to relive the experience by Tim's hospital bed, but I'm not proud of my attitude either. You see, I'm not as grateful as I thought I was, not as submissive to a sovereign God. It's for this reason that the subject of gratitude fascinates me and why I have taken time to research it in depth. In the words of one of my earlier books: discipleship matters.[3]

Peter Maiden
Kendal

1

'You owe me'

An entitlement is a provision made in accordance with a legal framework of a society. Typically, entitlements are based on concepts of principle ('rights') which are themselves based in concepts of social equality or enfranchisement.

In the 2000s, the meaning of the word has extended to encompass informal expectations of social relationships, social conventions and social norms which are considered unreasonable or unduly prescriptive upon others.[1]

Narcissism – an inflated view of the self – is everywhere. Public figures say it's what makes them stray from their wives. Parents teach it by dressing children in T-shirts that say 'Princess'. Teenagers and young adults hone it on Facebook, and celebrity newsmakers have elevated it to an art form. And it's what's making people depressed, lonely and buried under piles of debt.[2]

Why was I so shocked by my response in that hospital room? Why did I expect a better deal? This was something that I urgently needed to unpack.

For most of my life, I have been a runner. Now, this may sound bizarre to some, but running is, in fact, my favourite form of relaxation! For the past few years, living as I do on the edge of the English Lake District, I've absolutely loved running in the mountains, and I can be at the bottom of a fell within fifteen minutes. As someone who is 71 at the time of writing, describing what I do as running may be a slight exaggeration – it might be more accurately termed shuffling!

But a few months ago, for a seven-month period, I wasn't even able to shuffle because of a painful foot injury. One day, in my frustration, I thought, 'I have been running for fifty years, but how often have I thanked God for the health and fitness to do so?' I realized there is so much that, shamefully, I take for granted in my life – things that friends and colleagues in less materially driven parts of the world with fewer amenities would see as huge blessings.

Come with me to a small church made of corrugated iron in southern Nepal, where I was preaching on the strategy of Satan and illustrating my talk from the book of Job. We're told how Job's family is destroyed: 'a mighty wind swept in from the desert and struck the four corners of the house' (Job 1:19). Ironically and dramatically, while I was speaking, a storm rolled in, with a violent wind and hailstones, which the local newspaper described as being the size of golf balls. The lights went out and I didn't know what was happening. What could I do without power? There was no light with which to see my notes nor a loudspeaker for my voice to be heard above the incredible din of the hailstones on the metal roof. By contrast, my Nepalese brothers and sisters were not fazed for a moment: candles appeared immediately and a hymn began drowning out the noise of the hailstones. Impressive. I determined that when I got back home, I would seek to be more grateful for so much to which I believed myself entitled.

Sadly, this good resolution did not last. Some time later, I was sitting at the wheel of my faithful but rather ancient Vauxhall Vectra. It had transported me and my family for more than a quarter of a million miles, almost without a hitch. Now it was really showing its age and, whenever I set out on a journey, I was no longer sure whether or not it would transport me to my intended destination. I was feeling grumpy: with all the miles I had to travel to fulfil my preaching schedule, I surely deserved better than this, didn't I? The thousands of times I had turned the ignition key and the engine had fired successfully – and I had safely reached numerous destinations – failed to cross my mind.

Entitlement thinking did not just rule in the hospital room – it was alive and kicking in my trusty Vauxhall Vectra too.

The age of entitlement

Whether it's when I'm running in the Lake District, preaching overseas or driving to umpteen destinations, I realize how easily I slip into today's entitlement attitude and culture. Much has been written in magazine articles and blogs about 'millennial entitlement' and the expectations of Generation Z – I don't plan to add to that. The conditioning to 'think entitlement' begins early in life. Today, our children are continually fed the message that 'You can do whatever you want to do. You just need to believe in yourself and everything will be possible.'

It's great to encourage our children to achieve their full potential, but we know that most of them will not fulfil their dreams of being Premier League football stars or global pop sensations. If we fill our children's minds with unrealistic expectations, surely we are in danger of fomenting this

3

entitlement culture. Some social commentators are, unsurprisingly, defining our age as the 'age of entitlement'. Since the end of the Second World War, the standard of living in most Western nations has risen to levels of which our forefathers could never have dreamt. At the same time, the services offered by governments have increased to unprecedented levels. The taxes that we have been paying have not kept up with the cost of providing these services, to which we increasingly believe we are entitled.

To take away services from voters in democratic countries is perceived as an unpopular choice. So what happens? Governments borrow money from the taxpayers of tomorrow to cover the expenditure of today. Some governments are even having to borrow money not just to cover extra expenditure but also to pay the interest on money borrowed for that expenditure. Brave is the politician who raises his or her head above the parapet and says that the party should be over. Realistically, who is going to have the political courage to speak out?

This entitled way of thinking is also evident in the world of education and among Generation Z. Academics report that many students believe that they are entitled to receive good marks, whatever their attitude to work might be. Researchers at the University of California, Irvine, found that a third of students expected a B grade just for attending lectures and completing the required reading. Elaine Clift writes, 'A sense of entitlement pervades the academy; excellence be damned.'[3]

Was this sense of entitlement as pervasive among previous generations? I don't believe it was.

A powerful childhood memory is of my father coming home with his weekly wage packet. He would open the small envelope, take out the cash and then always do the same two things. First, he took from the cupboard what was known as 'the Lord's tin': into this went the tithe – 10 per cent of the money always put aside first to support Christian work, such as church and missionary endeavours. However tight things were financially, this was untouchable. Second, there was the holiday tin, in which he saved money to fund our two weeks off at the coast, 23 miles away. Borrowing was not an option – it was a bit questionable and not quite acceptable. If you did not have what you needed, then you waited until you did. For some items, we waited a very long time; with the waiting, the excitement increased and, I think, also the gratitude when it finally arrived. I still remember when we got our first television and, although I can't quite remember it, I know that the arrival of our first car was a red-letter day for the family.

But today's entitled consumer asks, 'Why wait? Life is too short,' although life expectancy has increased considerably since my parents' day. Credit is mostly easily available; debt is no longer socially unacceptable – it's even expected. My generation is accused of spending the hard-earned inheritance received from our industrious, frugal parents, who saved carefully, and of carelessly spending money we should be leaving to our children. Yet I know that many of us are determining how to lend or give money to help our children on to the property ladder.

There would not be much of a future for this consumer age if the attitude of the apostle Paul were to take hold. He wrote to his friends at Philippi, 'I have learned the secret of being content in any and every situation' (Philippians 4:12). This is a dangerous idea – for the consumer age to continue to thrive, we have to be continually convinced that we need more. Tony Walter argues that 'need' is the new religion.[4] Certainly, the shopping centre has replaced the church on Sunday as the popular place of choice. Consumerism promises to satisfy our needs in an unprecedented way, but it depends on satisfaction never quite being achieved.

Richard A. Easterlin asks, 'Will raising the incomes of all increase the happiness of all?' He continues:

> The answer to this question can now be given with somewhat greater assurance than at the turn of the [twentieth] century . . . It is 'no.' The conclusion is that there has been no improvement in happiness in the United States over almost a half century in which real GDP per capita more than doubled.[5]

Love Jesus or use him?

I have shown how easily I slip into entitlement thinking and I am certainly not the first follower of Christ to do so. The rich young ruler turned down the invitation to follow Jesus because he had 'great wealth' which he was unwilling to part with. 'Then Jesus said to his disciples, "I tell you the truth, it is very hard for a rich person to enter the Kingdom of Heaven"' (Matthew 19:23, NLT). Peter's response to this was: 'We have left everything to follow you! What then will there be for us?' (verse 27). Jesus was very gracious in his response to this rather selfish question, probably because these disciples had given up so much. However, after assuring them of a huge eternal return on their investment, he warned against a selfish spirit: 'But many who are first will be last, and many who are last will be first' (verse 30).

There is even a false teaching in the church today to support entitlement thinking: the advocates of what has become known as the prosperity gospel or Word of Faith movement assure us that we are entitled to health and wealth; they are part of the package of our salvation. Health and wealth are ours to receive by faith, for the atonement of Christ includes not just the removal of sin but also the removal of sickness and poverty. As Kenneth Copeland wrote in *The Laws of Prosperity*, 'Since God's covenant has been established and prosperity is a provision of the covenant, you need to realize that prosperity belongs to you now!'[6]

While we may not have been duped by this heresy, is it possible that this teaching may have influenced us in subtle ways? I often find that when things do not go well for us as Christians, we begin to be disappointed with God, doubting his love and even his ability to intervene. While you may not expect total health and prosperity all the time, do you think (as I did in that hospital ward) that, provided you are faithful to God, he is bound to be faithful to you and surely that means that things should basically go well for you?

Have you ever heard, or even said or thought, any of the following statements and questions?

- 'I've worked hard, improved my chances by getting
  an education, often at very inconvenient times. I can't
  understand why God doesn't provide me with a better-
  paid job.'
- 'I am so tired of being single, so frustrated. I have kept
  myself sexually pure, at least in deed, and I have been
  praying about this for years. Why doesn't God come
  through for me?'

- 'Children are a blessing from God, so why
am I struggling with infertility? After all, I only
want to be a godly parent. How can that be
wrong?'

Even if we're not struggling with specific issues such as these, don't we expect, at the very least, such blessings as reasonable health, financial provision, the ability to hold down a job, a basically happy marriage, a loving family and a caring church? Isn't there a danger that we think we love Jesus when we're actually *using* him, expecting him to turn up when we are sick or in need in some serious way? He is 'the big fix'. We expect an experience with him that will take away our pain and suffering. But if we are not careful, this begins to resemble the drug addict looking for a high or the drinker looking for that alcoholic haze to achieve at least a brief respite from pain. After all, we know Jesus, and when we know someone well, surely it entitles us to certain privileges? After all, when someone applies late for a place at a conference, the late application may not matter, if the organizer is a good friend. The friendship has its privileges and the individual expects the organizer to make an exception – just this once.

Nevertheless, that isn't how life works. Let's look at the story of Jacob and his descendants.

God spoke to Israel in a vision at night and said, 'Jacob, Jacob!'

'Here I am,' he replied.

'I am God, the God of your father,' he said. 'Do not be afraid to go down to Egypt, for I will make you into a

great nation there. I will go down to Egypt with you, and I will surely bring you back again.'
(Genesis 46:2–4)

So off Jacob and his family went in obedience to God. What was the result of their obedience? Four hundred years of suffering and slavery. God kept his promise completely. (Yes, you read that correctly.) He made them into a great nation, through all their suffering in Egypt, and he eventually brought them back to Canaan. But the purpose of God was not fulfilled without trial and suffering on the part of these people. In the New Testament Jesus said, 'In this world you will have trouble' (John 16:33). We are not entitled to an easy ride. God has made no such promises to us. He has promised us just what he promised to Jacob: I will be with you; I will fulfill all my purposes and promises and, eventually, in my time, I will deliver you.

> *'It is high time to stop thinking entitlement*
> *and to start thinking gift, privilege and grace.'*

It is high time to stop thinking entitlement and to start thinking gift, privilege and grace. Thanksgiving and praise will then begin to flow from our lives. Imagine for a moment that you were able to get everything you wanted in life. Would you ever thirst after Christ? Those unfulfilled desires remind us of where our ultimate satisfaction lies. As Augustine famously said, 'Our hearts are restless until they find their rest in thee.'[7]

9

Reflection

Read Psalm 73.

1 Does the honesty of Asaph stand out as he bluntly
   expresses his true feelings to God? There are no empty
   platitudes here. Not only are his words well chosen but
   there is also an expression of the reality of his heart.
   (a) Do you ever pray like this?
   (b) Do you believe that God is offended or pleased by
        such prayers?
2 Asaph begins by honouring God: surely he is good,
   especially to his chosen people and those who are seeking
   to be pure in heart.
   (a) But what does he see (verses 3–12)?
   (b) What is his initial response to what he sees
        (verses 2 and 13)?
   (c) Did Asaph believe that the people of God were
        entitled to something far different from what
        he sees?
3 How did Asaph eventually come to terms with the
   situation (verses 16–20)? Being in the sanctuary – the
   presence of God changed Asaph's whole perspective. He
   was able to take a long look rather than be overwhelmed
   by what he saw immediately around him.

2

Blessed

Gratitude leads us off the riverbank of If Only and escorts us onto the fertile valley of Already. The anxious heart says, 'Lord, if only I had this, that, or the other, I'd be okay.' The grateful heart says, 'Oh look! You've already given me this, that, and the other. Thank you, God.'[1]

More than thirty years ago, Win and I were travelling in Malaysia. It was a long, hard trip. Most days, the temperature and humidity made life very uncomfortable. We found eating the food so challenging that we were actually hoping there might be a McDonald's at the airport! We were missing our children and generally feeling sorry for ourselves – you get the picture.

It was just before Christmas, a season that Win loves (I often think we should charge people to come to look at our house when she has finished putting up the decorations). We couldn't wait to be home and, as the day approached, our excitement was rising. We were to board a flight to Kuala Lumpur from a small airport in central Malaysia and, from there, on to London and home.

You can imagine how we felt when we arrived at the local airport to find that the flight had been cancelled. With no more flights scheduled that day, we knew that we would miss the connecting flight home. We were told that overnight accommodation would be provided in a small hotel near the airport. Thirty years ago, not all the hotels in rural Asia were particularly comfortable, so in the taxi en route to the hotel, I prepared Win for the worst. What a pessimist I was: the hotel had a five-star rating, and it deserved every one of those stars. The Christmas decorations were magnificent, the restaurant offered beautiful Western and delicious Asian food and, with the financial compensation for the missed flight proving more than enough, no McDonald's was required!

Win and I got the opposite of what we were expecting and, because we were flying 'bucket-shop' economy prices, I didn't think we deserved to be treated as well as we were. But we certainly enjoyed it. I should add that when Paul wrote that he had learnt to be content whatever the circumstances, he was not saying that he could just handle poverty – he could also handle riches when they came his way!

Blessed by a king's generosity

Mephibosheth was the grandson of King Saul in the Old Testament. He was just five years old when the tragic news arrived that his father Jonathan and his grandfather had been killed in battle. In the moments of panic that followed, his nurse, who had picked him up to run for their lives, unfortunately dropped him: he was disabled for the rest of his life. And he was not only physically disabled, he was also politically disabled. Most dynasties in the Near East were wiped out when new ones emerged, so he seemed to be completely without security.

Mephibosheth was probably emotionally disabled as well; his self-esteem was completely shattered. The Bible records that he described himself as 'a dead dog' (2 Samuel 9:8). The best he could hope for was to keep his head down and live quietly, if always anxiously, in a place called Lo Debar. He must have feared the knock on the door, signalling that his whereabouts had finally been revealed to the authorities. He might have wondered if his disability could at least save his life. After all, he was unlikely to be any threat to the new dynasty.

One day the dreaded knock did come and he was summoned to the palace. What was racing through his mind as he made his way there? Was this the end of his liberty or even his life?

It was a journey that would change his life for ever. As the reality for Win and me in Malaysia turned out to be the polar opposite of what we expected, so did events for Mephibosheth. No-one could have prepared him for what he was about to hear. Instead of encountering a vengeful monarch breathing threats and desiring angry retribution, he met a king who wanted to give him one blessing after another. David desired to do so for the sake of his friend Jonathan (see 2 Samuel 9:1). Mephibosheth received unmerited favour as an act of generosity and kindness.

Blessed for Jesus' sake

As someone who, along with the rest of humanity, has sinned and 'fallen short of the glory of God' (Romans 3:23), I am entitled to nothing but the judgment of God. Yet I find myself receiving the very opposite of what I deserve. When I look back over more than seven decades of life, the word that readily comes to my mind is 'blessed'. I have certainly received what I did not deserve: blessing instead of judgment. For most of my life, I have known Jesus Christ as my Saviour and have experienced, year after year, the mercy, goodness and generosity of God. I have lived a life of grace, for God's grace has been my constant experience. God has poured out his grace, and continues to do so for me, and not because I deserved mercy.

> *'I have lived a life of grace, for God's grace has*
> *been my constant experience.'*

Just as Mephibosheth was blessed by David for Jonathan's sake, I have been blessed by God for Jesus' sake. His purpose in saving and keeping me is that I might give glory to Jesus. Does this mean that life has been easy? Far from it. I have already mentioned some of our family challenges and you will discover more as you continue to read. There have been ministry crises, even as I have been blessed with the responsibility for leading several Christian organizations. There have been failures in both my life and my leadership. But, as I look back, the overwhelming picture is one of God's undeserved blessing. Truly, I have been a recipient of grace.

If you are a believer, you too have lived a blessed life. You might disagree. You might say that life has been a struggle, even filled with sorrows. For many people that is the case. But imagine life without the knowledge of Christ and the salvation you have found in him, and without the presence of the Holy Spirit as your constant companion. Imagine life with no future hope to look forward to.

In the New Testament, Paul's life was far from easy. His ministry was physically, emotionally and spiritually demanding. He was persecuted by unbelievers who hated his message and he was often misunderstood by believers. This is how he felt when he wrote to the church in Corinth: 'We are hard pressed on every side, but not crushed; perplexed, but not in despair; persecuted, but not abandoned; struck down, but not destroyed' (2 Corinthians 4:8–9). Despite his trials, he knew that he was a thoroughly blessed man. He writes to the Ephesians, 'Praise be to the God and Father of our Lord Jesus Christ, who has blessed us in the heavenly realms with every spiritual blessing in Christ' (Ephesians 1:3).

Overwhelmed by blessings

Take a few minutes to read Ephesians 1:3–14. Paul was so overwhelmed by the blessing he had received that he didn't stop for breath when he dictated these words. Imagine his secretary trying to keep up with him as the words gushed from his lips. For Paul, his transformation had been dramatic. He was just outside Damascus, about his business of defending Judaism and dealing with the problematic, growing sect of Jesus followers. But, before he got into the city, his life was forever changed as he spoke with Jesus Christ, whom he had been convinced was dead. His transformation was immediate, dramatic and complete.

My situation was very different. I was taught the way of Christ on my mother's knee and became a follower of Jesus at a very young age. Although I can remember many days when I have not loved Jesus as I should, I cannot recall a day when I did not love him. But I too have received everything that Paul is thanking God for in this Ephesians passage. Whatever way you came to faith, the truths of this chapter are for you too. They are the permanent, secure blessings for every believer. It is my prayer that all believers can share the excitement that Paul was so clearly experiencing.

The Trinity and a flow of blessing

Father, Son and Holy Spirit – the Trinity – are involved in this flow of blessing. The source of the flow is God the Father himself. He 'has blessed us in the heavenly realms with every spiritual blessing' (Ephesians 1:3). Christ is the pool of blessings in which we bathe; it is 'in Christ' that we enjoy them; they exist because of our union with him. They are 'spiritual blessings', writes John Stott, 'a phrase which may well mean "every blessing of the Holy Spirit".'[2] They are from the Father, in the Son and through the Holy Spirit. The triune God has one intention and that is to bless us. The blessings are due to his will (verses 5, 9 and 11), his pleasure (verses 5 and 9), his grace (verse 6), his blood (verse 7), his purpose (verse 9) and for his glory (verses 12 and 14). It is entirely his initiative that leads to our being his sons and daughters (verse 5). Chosen by the Father, redeemed through the Son and sealed by the Holy Spirit.

Super rich and super blessed

So God has blessed us with 'every spiritual blessing in the heavenly places' (verse 3, NASB). Paul refers to the heavenly places four more times in the letter (1:20; 2:6; 3:10; 6:12). We are living in this fallen world with all its pressures, temptations and disappointments, but we are living here the life of the world to come. We are citizens of heaven because of all that God has done for us in Christ (Philippians 3:20). As Paul wrote these words, he was under house arrest, handcuffed to a Roman soldier, but the walls and the handcuffs did not limit his horizons.

This life of blessing is rich only if we can appreciate all that we possess. In Ephesians, Paul writes of the 'riches of [Christ's] grace' (Ephesians 2:7), 'the riches of his glorious inheritance' (1:18), 'the unsearchable riches of Christ' (3:8, ESV) and 'the riches of his glory' (Philippians 4:19).

In fact, we have it all: 'every spiritual blessing' is ours. We don't have to wait for further experiences or for deeper truths to be revealed. Everything the Holy Spirit has to give us he has already given us in Christ. It will take us the rest of our lives to grow into all that is available to us, but there is no reason for any delay on that journey into fullness of life in him (Colossians 2:10).

We recognized earlier that the Christian life can be tough. We are at war in the spiritual realm, so we should not expect life to be a picnic. But, even in the heat of the battle, the blessings Paul points out to the Ephesians remain secure. A vital point of this book is that these blessings are permanent – no-one can steal them from us. Although Satan continually seeks to spoil our enjoyment of them, he cannot rob us of them.

Amazing grace

Let us watch the God who loves to bless in action.

Jesus is in Sychar in Samaria; he is tired after the journey from Judea, so he sits down beside a well (John 4:6). It is early evening; his disciples have gone into Sychar to buy food. As he sits waiting, a Samaritan woman comes to draw water. Instead of ignoring her or moving away to a respectable distance, he engages her in conversation. He asks her for a drink and she is clearly taken by surprise: 'The Samaritan woman said to him, "You are a Jew and I am a Samaritan woman. How can you ask me for a drink?"' (verse 9). Jesus is breaking all the social conventions. As a Jew, his being in

Samaria at all was a surprise, but talking to a woman in public, especially to *this* woman, is very unusual. This woman has a reputation; she has worked her way through five husbands and is now living with another man. She is probably despised in the community, the object of gossip and disdain. How will Jesus treat her and, if he speaks to her, what will his message be? Will he join the chorus of condemnation?

Jesus says to her, 'If you knew the gift of God and who it is that asks you for a drink, you would have asked him and he would have given you living water' (verse 10). In other words, if only she could realize it, God has a gift for her and Jesus, God's Son, is sitting right beside her. So rather than condemn her, God wants to bless her. In fact, all three members of the Trinity are again involved in bringing divine blessing to this woman: God the Father wants to give her a gift; God the Son is sitting beside her telling her about the gift; and the gift itself, this living water, is the Holy Spirit. If she is ready to deal with her sin (for surely that is why Jesus brings up the matter of her husbands in verse 16), then God stands ready to bless her with the gift of his Spirit to quench her thirsty soul.

When the disciples return from buying food, they are surprised ('shocked' is used in the New Living Translation) to find their teacher talking to her (verse 27). Jesus is making a huge statement about prejudice. By his actions, he is declaring himself to be the Messiah for all people.

That is the God we worship, a God who longs to bless us. His promise from the earliest days was to bring blessing to every nation on earth (Genesis 12:3). This has also been my experience, which is why I want to grow in thankfulness and encourage you to do the same. It is not because we are entitled, it's because we know amazing grace. We receive, and will continue to receive for all eternity, what we really don't deserve.

> *'It is not because we are entitled,*
> *it's because we know amazing grace.'*

Reflection

Read Psalm 103 and Psalm 104.

These two psalms show how God has blessed his people and the planet on which he has placed us. We will focus specifically on Psalm 103 here.

1 David is encouraging himself to bless the Lord because of who he is and for all the blessings he receives from God's hand. Notice that true worship involves the commitment and use of all our faculties: 'all my inmost being, praise his holy name'. Worship is not a mindless spiritual high.
2 To 'praise his holy name' is to praise God for who he is – his majestic character. As you read through the psalm, identify some of the characteristics or attributes of God that stimulate David's praise.
3 Read through the psalm again and look for the 'benefits' David has received from God.
4 Remember the warning, particularly when you are facing hard times, not to 'forget all his benefits'.

3

A debtor

Thankfulness to God is a recognition that God, in his goodness and faithfulness, has provided for us and cared for us, both physically and spiritually. It is a recognition that we are totally dependent upon him, and that all that we are and have comes from God.[1]

There are warning signs that you can look out for which indicate that you are moving from being God-dependent to self-sufficient. One of these is arrogance or pride.[2]

I was out walking with my son and, stopping at a shop, he spotted something he wanted. Conveniently, he had left his money at home, something which happened rather regularly! I lent him a few pounds and he later asked, 'Dad, how much do I owe you?' In jest I responded, 'Never forget you owe me everything – you wouldn't be here without me!'

Self-made or dependent?

Bart Simpson (a character from the US animated series *The Simpsons*), by contrast, has no sense of indebtedness. He prays before supper, 'Dear God, we paid for all this stuff ourselves, so thanks for nothing.'[3] He prides himself, as many do today, on being self-made. Two posters that I recently spotted also portray this prevalent world view. The first enthused, 'The greatest thing in the world is to know how to be self-sufficient.'

The second claimed, 'Self-sufficiency is the greatest of all wealth.' Dependence is seen as weakness; in other words: 'Stand up for yourself; no-one is going to do it for you.'

At this point, I want to say that I am unashamedly dependent, and I love it. I am not alone, for it doesn't all depend on me, or even on me and all those who might encourage and help me, although I am grateful to the many who have had that ministry in my life. The God who made me is there for me – always there for me – every day and even every night.

Take a moment to drink in the words of Psalm 121:

I lift up my eyes to the mountains –
    where does my help come from?
My help comes from the LORD,
    the Maker of heaven and earth.

He will not let your foot slip –
    he who watches over you will not slumber;
indeed, he who watches over Israel
    will neither slumber nor sleep.

The LORD watches over you –
    the LORD is your shade at your right hand;
the sun will not harm you by day,
    nor the moon by night.

The LORD will keep you from all harm –
    he will watch over your life;
the LORD will watch over your coming and going
    both now and for evermore.

As well as my dependence, I recognize my indebtedness. The US author and speaker John Piper writes:

> All we deserve from God is judgment [as noted earlier] . . . Therefore, every breath we take, every time our heart beats, every day that the sun rises, every moment we see with our eyes or hear with our ears or speak with our mouths or walk with our legs, is for now a free and undeserved gift to sinners who only deserve judgment.
>
> I say 'for now' because if you refuse to see God in his gifts, they will turn out not to be gifts at all, but high court evidence of ingratitude . . .
>
> But for those who see the merciful hand of God in every breath they take and give credit where it is due, Jesus Christ will be seen and evoked as the great purchaser of every undeserved breath. Every heartbeat will be received as a gift from his hand.[4]

Although dependence and indebtedness are seen as weakness in an age of self-sufficiency, Jesus said, 'Apart from me you can do nothing' and 'I am the vine; you are the branches' (John 15:5). Without the life that comes from the vine, we have nothing to give. This understanding is countercultural but, as Christians, we delight in our dependence and indebtedness. As we praise God and as we pray to him, we express this. We are saying in effect, 'I need you.' We don't say it with feelings of failure and regret but in the certain knowledge that this is how God created us to be, and that it is a privilege to live in this way.

When I was in that hospital room with my son (see the introduction), although I was desperate and even at times angry that God was allowing Tim's suffering, I knew that I was not alone. Similarly, while I was leading the ministry of Operation Mobilisation, there were times when OM was right on the edge. We purchased four ships over the years, and ships are obviously not cheap! Staged payments were often required for refitting these vessels; we endured the nail-biting experience of a deadline getting closer, sometimes with more than £1 million to pay but nothing in the bank. We were utterly dependent on God and his people, and that's the point here – we knew we were not alone: God was with us and had called us to this initiative, and thousands of his people around the world were standing with us in faith. We were attempting big things; it would have been so easy for pride to set in but, as we met to pray, with the deadline looming large, we were constantly reminded just how completely dependent we were. It was a safe place to be and, as we saw God provide again and again, we expressed praise and thanks to the God whom dependent people could entirely trust.

A huge barrier to gratitude is our failure to understand just how dependent we are. If we realize we are constantly dependent and indebted, then it is going to knock any sense of entitlement firmly on the head. If we believe something is our right, by contrast, then we are not going to be thankful when we receive it. But if we realize something is a gift, undeserved and unearned, then thanks will surely follow.

> 'A huge barrier to gratitude is our failure
> to understand just how dependent we are.'

So just how dependent are we? In 1 Corinthians 4:7, Paul asks the church a huge question: 'What do you have that you did not receive?' The Christians there were squabbling. God designed the church to be a single body, but the Corinthians' actions had chopped it into many parts. Factions had emerged, with some saying, 'We follow Paul', while others sided with Apollos, still others with Cephas (Peter), and then there were the super-spiritual who said they were above such things, for they were siding with Christ himself! They imagined themselves to be so wise. How much more sensible to follow the eloquent Apollos than the stuttering Paul. Paul effectively said to them: 'Who on earth do you think you are, coming to such conclusions, thinking it's all down to your superior wisdom?' Or, in other words: 'What do you have that you did not receive?'

Any true wisdom that we may have is not down to us: it's a gift; it's grace; it's from God.

All a gift

Do we really believe that? Everything we are and everything that is of any value in our lives is given to us. These gifts are not things for us to be proud of, not things that ever allow us any right to look down on others. The only place to look is up to God, with thankful hearts.

It was God who breathed into us the breath of life. Paul expresses it plainly when speaking in Athens: 'He himself gives everyone life and breath and everything else' (Acts 17:25). Every single day we live is a gift from God to treasure. 'This is the day that the LORD has made; let us rejoice and be glad in it' (Psalm 118:24, ESV). There may be some hard things that we will have to face in the day ahead, but God has given it to us. He has given it to us because he loves us and, as we shall see later in this book, even the most difficult things we face can be a cause for thanksgiving to our God.

I am writing this particular chapter in Canada. It's autumn – 'the fall', as they call it here. The trees are stunning – so stunning that as I was driving my grandchildren to school this morning, I was in danger of being distracted by their sheer beauty. One of the reasons why God gave me the gift of this day was to enjoy that beauty. Another, of course, was to enjoy four of my grandchildren, even when they had a significant falling out in the back of the car. Can you pay for these kinds of things, Bart Simpson?

How about the new life we have as believers in Christ? Can you pay for that? Through human rebellion that gift of life was lost. God said, 'To dust you will return' (Genesis 3:19). It was a death sentence but, such is the love and mercy of our generous God that, the moment the death sentence was issued, plans for a fresh gift of new life were laid. And another death sentence was issued: the seed of the woman, Jesus, would crush the head of the serpent, Satan. But the only way his head, his power, could be crushed was through the death of Jesus. Through his death, the agent of death would eventually be destroyed. Glorious new life would again flow because of the victory of our Lord Jesus. He made clear his purpose as our Rescuer. 'I have come that they may have life, and have it to the full' (John 10:10). That new, full life could not flow to us without the gift of his own life. Paul would later write, 'Thanks be to God for his indescribable gift!' (2 Corinthians 9:15). Indescribable, indeed.

Permanent blessings

These are some of the permanent blessings on which we focused in the last chapter. They are the result of the finished work of Christ and, once we have received them, they cannot be lost. They are not based on our own attempts at righteousness but, rather, through faith, we express our dependence on Christ's perfect righteousness and the fact that his death pays the penalty for all our unrighteousness. To understand the core message of this book, you must understand and, by faith, accept this truth. The death and resurrection of Jesus have changed everything: death was the result of human sin, but life is the result of Christ's sacrifice. The gifts of God's forgiveness, his permanent presence in our lives through his indwelling Holy Spirit, and complete future certainty are ours now and for ever. My gratitude is not based on feelings but rooted firmly in historical realities: the life, death and resurrection of Jesus, which remain unchanged through all my changing moods.

Roger and June had worshipped and served the Lord Jesus for a lifetime, both in the UK and abroad. They were now well into their eighties, and the news wasn't good. Roger's cancer had returned and he had also been diagnosed with vascular dementia. You might think my phone call to them would have been a difficult one. But when I asked how they were, June answered, 'Peter, we have so much to be thankful for. God is so good.' June was not being unrealistic and, as the conversation continued, we went on to talk about the very real challenges they were facing. But they were equally real about their experience of God's goodness. They were rejoicing in those permanent gifts that they had received from the hand of God. Their experience of these gifts countered, indeed outweighed, the challenges that had recently confronted them. And they knew that the latter were not permanent. A day would come when they would both be completely disease-free for ever.

Those who see themselves as self-made successes are not likely to live thankful lives. You must be thankful to someone and being thankful to yourself would, I think, seem strange, even to the most independent individuals. Those who start the day recognizing that all their waking breaths are a gift from God, and that everything of value they enjoy flows from a good and generous God, will only grow in thankfulness and praise.

Reflection

Read Psalm 61.

We can't be absolutely sure when David wrote this psalm. It is possible that he wrote it when he was fleeing from his son Absalom's rebellion. How desperate these days were for him is described in 2 Samuel 15:13–37.

1 David's greatest desire was to 'be in [God's] tent for ever and take refuge in the shelter of [his] wings' (verse 4). He had always loved the presence of God, but the trials he was enduring only served to increase his longing to be in the Lord's presence. David knew he was nothing without God. This psalm expresses David's utter dependence
on God and his discomfort and distress when he was separated from his presence. In the first verse of Psalm 62, he is clear: 'My soul finds rest in God alone.'

2 Note that David mentions the specific blessings that God has brought into his life.

3 These were hard days for David, but they were surely vitally important days too, confirming his need to rely utterly on God.

4 Can you look back on hard but significant days that you have had? Review them and remind yourself of the lessons you have learnt.

4

Ingratitude but choosing gratitude

The greatest sufferer that lives in this world of redeeming love, and who has the offer of heaven before him, has cause of gratitude.[1]

'Unclean!'

That is what someone with leprosy at the time of Christ had to call out if there was any danger of accidental contact with another human being. The disease was disfiguring and fatal. Physical isolation was demanded but there was a psychological isolation too, which must have been equally difficult to deal with. Leprosy was considered to be defiling and sufferers were ashamed. And, with no way of earning a living, they were totally dependent on others for their very survival.

One day, as Jesus walked into a village, ten men who had leprosy met him. They couldn't come near him, of course, but they could shout, 'Jesus, Master, have pity on us!' (Luke 17:13). They didn't mention leprosy, and Jesus didn't mention healing. His instruction to them was to 'Go, show yourselves to the priest' (verse 14), the health inspector of the day (see Leviticus 14:2). Was this a test of their faith? It would seem so, for 'as they went, they were cleansed' (verse 14).

How can we even begin to imagine the joy, the relief, they experienced the moment the priest declared them to be free of leprosy? Their death sentence was annulled at a stroke. Surely their first move would be to find Jesus, their only concern to know how to thank the person who had done this for them. What words could possibly express their gratitude? But no. Remarkably, thanks was the exception, not the rule. 'One of them, when he saw he was healed, came back, praising God in a loud voice. He threw himself at Jesus' feet and thanked him – and he was a Samaritan' (verses 15–16). Only one.

Jesus asks three questions: 'Were not all ten cleansed? Where are the other nine? Was no-one found to return and give praise to God except this foreigner?' (verses 17–18). Jesus expresses surprise on two counts: first, that only one of those healed returned to express thanks; and, second, that the only one who did was a Samaritan, a foreigner who would usually have had nothing to do with a Jew.

Ingratitude in the garden

The story of the ten lepers presents a shocking case of ingratitude, but is it really so shocking when we consider the whole of human history?

We have been struggling with ingratitude from the very beginning of time. A lack of thankfulness lay at the root of our original rebellion against God. He provided lavishly for his creation but, instead of thanking and honouring him for his goodness, Adam and Eve were dissatisfied. They wanted more and, as we face the continual challenge of our consumer age in which 'more' seems to be the defining word, it looks as if nothing much has changed down through time.

Adam and Eve's dissatisfaction led them to bow to Satan's suggestions rather than obey God's instructions, and to believe the lie that God isn't good after all. Satan convinced them that God did not really want the best for them: wasn't God keeping things from them rather than supplying everything they needed? Satan promised them that they would be like God if they rebelled, despite the fact that they were *already* made in the image and likeness of God. Their choice to disobey had its root in ingratitude. It is not just that ingratitude is sinful but that sin, at its core, is an act of ingratitude. Martin Luther said, 'Now take note of the order of the stages of perdition. The first is ingratitude or the failure to be grateful.'[2]

But we can go even further back than the Garden of Eden. The fall of Lucifer also had its roots in ingratitude, an unwillingness to honour God and bow to his will. Lucifer, dissatisfied with his exalted position among the angels, wanted more: 'I will make myself like the Most High' (Isaiah 14:14). He used the same temptation to pride to bring down Adam and Eve. God had said death would result if they disobeyed him by eating of the tree of the knowledge of good and evil (Genesis 2:17), but Satan countered: 'You will not surely die . . . For God knows that when you eat of it your eyes will be opened, and you will be like God, knowing good and evil' (3:4–5, NIV84).

Ingratitude among the Israelites

Ingratitude would also become the root cause of the persistent sinful failure and continual frustration of the children of Israel, as grumbling would become their default position. It was not just the occasional minor complaint that was soon forgotten either, but evidence of the desperate spiritual state into which they had fallen. They had personally experienced so much of the power and goodness of the God who was committed by covenant to them: deliverance from bondage in Egypt, the crossing of the Red Sea and the vanquishing of their enemy. Even so, soon after these miraculous interventions, they were doubting whether God was still with them and whether he had the power to help them. On receiving the reports of those who had reconnoitred the land that God had promised to them, they chose to believe the negative ones rather than the God-honouring, faith-filled reports of Joshua and Caleb:

> That night all the people of the community raised their voices and wept aloud. All the Israelites grumbled against Moses and Aaron, and the whole assembly said to them, 'If only we had died in Egypt! Or in this desert! Why is the Lord bringing us to this land only to let us fall by the sword? Our wives and children will be taken as plunder. Wouldn't it be better for us to go back to Egypt?' And they said to each other, 'We should choose a leader and go back to Egypt.'
> (Numbers 14:1–4)

Called to bring glory to God through their faithfulness to him, to become a light to the nations, the Israelites instead dishonoured him with their ingratitude and unbelief. Their grumbling revealed their abject spiritual state.

In the New Testament, Paul would show this link between ingratitude and dishonouring God. 'For although they knew God, they neither glorified him as God nor gave thanks to him, but their thinking became futile and their foolish hearts were darkened' (Romans 1:21). Albert Mohler writes,

'Thanksgiving is a deeply theological act.'[3] Honouring God as God leads us naturally to gratitude. Believing that God is our God who is 'for' us – that he is good, that he is great, that he will certainly fulfil the good promises he has made – has to be foundational. By contrast, ingratitude, at its heart, is atheistic: Paul warns the believers in Rome that it leads to idolatry, futile thinking and foolishness.

Be on your guard

Ingratitude is a vice which we should continually be on the lookout for today.

Writing to Timothy about the last days, that period in which we live, between the first and second comings of Christ, Paul lists ingratitude as being one of the characteristics of this age. As you read the list Paul gives of human characteristics in the last days, consider how many of them are linked with ingratitude:

> People will be lovers of themselves, lovers of money, boastful, proud, abusive, disobedient to their parents, ungrateful, unholy, without love, unforgiving, slander- ous, without self-control, brutal, not lovers of the good, treacherous, rash, conceited, lovers of pleasure rather than lovers of God.
> (2 Timothy 3:2–4)

Looking back over decades of leadership in a missionary organization, a local church and several other Christian charities, I have come to the sad conclusion that we can all too often be a thankless lot! It is much easier to concentrate on the problem or the failure than to celebrate the success.

*'It is much easier to concentrate
on the problem or the failure than
to celebrate the success.'*

Keswick Ministries is a Christian charity which, among many other things, organizes a Bible convention each year in the beautiful English Lake District town of Keswick. It attracts up to fifteen thousand people over a three-week period. I had the privilege of chairing the council for several years and, after each convention, I would receive a number of letters and emails. Some were positive, expressing thanks to God and to those who had worked hard to deliver the convention, but more were negative.

It was surprising what some people could find to complain about; often it was the volume of the music played by the band leading sung worship. For some, it was too loud while, for others, too soft – they wanted the volume considerably increased. One gentleman wrote regularly to complain that a harp was not part of the music provided. Well, I suppose he needed to harp on about something! Some of the criticism was constructive and was used over time to improve the convention. Often, though, improving the convention did not seem to be the motive of the correspondent. Rather, he or she had been upset and wanted us to know that.

One real sadness of being involved in Christian work for more than fifty years is witnessing a number of leaders I have met being gradually worn down by grumbling and complaining. Often the complainant will mention something that's not going well in the life of the church or organization but will make no comment on all that is going well. Ingratitude drives people out of Christian ministry – yes, it's that

40

serious – and that's the very opposite of how things should be. We must be ready to give and receive positive criticism but we must be readier still to express our thanks to those who serve us well, affirming others rather than undermining them and forgiving quickly when mistakes are made.

That's how it should be and, yet, I myself fall into ingratitude and complaint so easily. For example, when I am asked to preach at a church, I want to know how much time has been allocated for the sermon and I plan to stick to it. I easily become critical if my time is squeezed because the rest of the service hasn't been well planned. I become grumpy and think, 'I have given many hours to sermon preparation. I have come a long way and have a long way to go home after the service.' You can imagine my attitude when I finally reach the podium! If I can only stop grumbling, lift my eyes and look around the church, I can see so much to be thankful for: individuals who have been helped through the ministry; the many volunteers giving freely of their time; every person with a story of grace to share.

In a fallen world where – without the gracious intervention of God through his Son, Jesus Christ, our only future would have been judgment – we now find ourselves blessed beyond words, surely there will always be reason for gratitude. We need only to open our eyes and look at what God is doing in his world, redeeming a fallen creation; we need only to look within and recognize that, with all our struggles and failures, his divine hand is at work.

Surely there are a thousand more reasons for thanksgiving than for grumbling or complaint?

Reflection

Read Psalm 78.

This is the second longest of the psalms but well worth reading carefully. Asaph is delivering a history lesson: the history of God's faithful, consistent dealing with his covenant people, and their history of grumbling, continual lack of contentment and rebellion in response.

1 Take a few minutes to note the comprehensive way in which God provided for and protected his people. Look at the verses beginning with the word 'he'.
2 The grumbling unbelief of the Lord's people is astonishing. It is expressed most starkly in verses 17–20. As you read through the psalm, can you see any reasons for this unbelief?
3 Examine your heart. Is there a grumbling attitude? Do you think more about the things you don't have than the continual flow of provision and protection from God's good hand?

5

Disciplined gratitude, not grudging submission

> Here is one of the most beautiful fruits of grace – a heart that is content, more given to worship than demand, and more given to the joy of gratitude than the anxiety of want.[1]

Roger and June, whom you met on page 31, had an important decision to make. Not only was Roger's health poor, their daughter was also battling cancer. How easy it would have been for them to become disappointed and dejected, and quite possibly bitter. But they chose instead to be thankful, concentrating on the huge, permanent gifts they had received, and were continuing to receive, from their generous Father God. They did not deny the bad news coming their way – they wept about it and, no doubt, it got them down from time to time – but those permanent gifts would live on, unlike the temporary blows and bad news.

A holy habit

Gratitude cannot be left to the mercy of our emotions.

God commands us as his people to give him praise and thanks, an exhortation that runs throughout the Bible. That should not surprise us. Whenever I think of God, his goodness springs readily to my mind. That is why we 'enter

his gates with thanksgiving and his courts with praise'
(Psalm 100:4).

David was sure that 'goodness and love' would follow him
'all the days' of his life (Psalm 23:6). The great Baptist preacher
Charles Spurgeon wrote:

> These twin guardian angels will always be with me. Just
> as when great princes go abroad and must not go un-
> attended, so it is with the believer. Goodness and mercy
> ['love' in the New International Version] follow him
> always – on the black days as well as the bright days.[2]

For more than seventy years, through all the highs and lows,
I have known the presence of those two 'angels'.

When you get the kind of bombshell that Roger and June
received, you cannot just push a button for gratitude to
overrule your concerns and fears. Gratitude must become a
way of life, a holy habit that you learn to develop over time.

Overflow

In Colossians 2:6–7 Paul writes, 'So then, just as you received
Christ Jesus as Lord, continue to live in him . . . strengthened
in the faith as you were taught, and overflowing with
thankfulness.' The way we received Christ is the way we must
continue to live in him each day.

Can you remember your thankfulness when you received
Christ and gradually began to understand all that you had
in him? Don't allow that thankfulness to disappear. Keep
reminding yourself of all that Christ has done, and continues to do, for you. You received him as Lord, submitting
yourself to his rule over your life. It was not a grudging

submission – you received him joyfully; to live under his rule and protection was an honour. That is where you live each day, a place of safety and huge privilege, and, as we have seen, it is not down to your intelligence or goodness but to his grace.

> *'It was not a grudging submission –*
> *you received him joyfully; to live under*
> *his rule and protection was an honour.'*

Gratitude cannot be isolated. Rather, it is the overflow of the life of a committed Christ follower. And others will receive from this overflow too. When I phoned Roger and June, my faith was strengthened and my praise of God well and truly stimulated by the overflow of their gratitude.

Respond well

You lose your job unexpectedly. How will you respond? Panic? Disappointment? Anger? You might experience all those emotions and many more besides. But what if you have learned over the years to bring all such emotions to your Father whom you know to be good? In his presence, you are reminded that you live under his lordship. You can commit your ways to the One whom you have chosen to rule your life; he is the King of kings and Lord of lords. Losing a job is serious; it can be devastating, but this deeper realization certainly alters your perspective.

Your passion is to be 'strengthened in the faith' and, although it may be very hard to appreciate it at the time, you might just see that this apparent disaster could become an opportunity for growth. What are you going to learn about God and yourself through this experience? Losing your job has not been followed by losing any of those generous permanent gifts from your Father, has it? At this moment, you might not have a job, but you are still in the hands of a good God: you still have salvation, the presence of your Saviour in the person of his Holy Spirit and the absolute certainty of your eternal inheritance. It is just possible that, even in the storm, you might be able to cry out a faltering but faith-filled thanksgiving:

> Father, I thank you that you are Lord of this and of every situation. I thank you that I can trust you in this moment. I believe my faith can be strengthened rather than weakened as I work through this issue with you at my side.

Gratitude can become your default position.

Sing for joy

It was more than fifty years ago, but I can still remember it vividly: my first experience of serving as a missionary with Operation Mobilisation. Little did I know that it would lead to a lifetime of ministry with the organization.

I was part of a team serving God for three months in Spain. There were about twenty of us and I was the only one who did not speak Spanish. I was lonely, and the team had very little money and not even much food to eat. My bed (if you could call it that) was a square of cardboard on a wooden floor. It was the perfect setting for a pity party. I was miserable and I remained miserable for quite a few days. In fact, the first month of the three was completely ruined by my attitude.

Then, one day, I went off on my own with a Bible and a hymn book. I had decided that my mood must change. It was not glorifying to God, not helpful to the rest of the team, and certainly no witness to any Spaniards looking on and taking note. I found a quiet place, as far away from people as I could get, and began to sing songs of praise from the hymn book. Then, with a concordance, I read through all the references to thankfulness I could find in Scriptures; gradually, my mood changed. I look back on the two months that followed as some of the most formative in my Christian life.

What was I up to? Was this a mental game – a case of mind over matter? No, I was speaking truth – the truth of God – to myself. I was reminding myself of those permanent gifts of God based on historical realities: the life, death and resurrection of Jesus, which remained forever unchanged through all my changing moods.

I wasn't the first person to battle through difficulties with the weapon of song. In the New Testament, Paul and Silas were in much greater difficulty than anything I experienced in Spain. After being severely flogged and thrown into prison in Philippi, they prayed and sang hymns to God (Acts 16:25). Suddenly a violent earthquake shook the place. All that happened led to the jailer and his family finding faith in Christ in the midst of shock and anguish.

My singing in Spain was not followed by anything as dramatic as an earthquake, but it certainly resulted in a total internal transformation from complaint to praise. My Spanish experience of thanksgiving was a sort of emergency measure, but how much better it would be if we can cultivate thanksgiving as a way of life, so that it becomes our default attitude instead.

Three times in three verses, Paul urges the Christians in Colosse to this thankful way of life (Colossians 3:15–17): 'Be thankful' (verse 15); 'singing to God with gratitude in your hearts' (verse 16); 'giving thanks to God the Father through him' (verse 17). Here, Paul is addressing a young church under threat from false teachers who were suggesting that their salvation was incomplete. As has always been the case with so many false teachers through the ages, they were trying to encourage a sense of restlessness among the believers, saying in effect: 'Your faith is at such an elementary level. It is good to follow Christ but you must go further. You need what we have to really have "fullness" in Christ.' Paul is adamant that, in Christ, the Colossian believers have all that they need: 'For in Christ all the fullness of the Deity lives in bodily form, and you have been given fullness in Christ, who is the Head over every power and authority' (Colossians 2:9–10, NIV84). Yes, they needed to grow in their knowledge and experience of Christ, which is true for us all, but rather than a restlessness, there must be a thankfulness, as we allow the peace and the word of Christ to rule and dwell in us.

So cultivating this habit of gratitude involves discipline. It is a deliberate choice we must make; it is the overflow of letting the word of Christ dwell in our hearts and resisting the suggestions of Satan. As we develop this godly habit, it can pervade everything we do; we can only imagine the joy that we will experience and the praise of God that will result.

Exercise

Determine to do something today to begin or develop a habit of gratitude in your life. Here are some suggestions:

1 Take a few moments in the morning, the middle of the day and the evening to stop, look back and remember those things that have taken place for which you should be grateful.
2 Begin a thanksgiving journal. At the close of each day, write down at least one thing you have been grateful for that day.
3 Each day or each week, come together as a family or in a small group for the express purpose of sharing your stories of gratitude.

If you want to study a psalm, look at Psalm 42 and note the magnificent struggle of the psalmist to throw off his imminent depression and place his hope in God.

6

Time out to remember

Be thankful. God has commanded it – for our good and for His glory. God's command to be thankful is not the threatening demand of a tyrant. Rather, it is the invitation of a lifetime – the opportunity to draw near to Him at any moment of the day.[1]

I am writing this chapter at the start of a three-day break with Win in a log cabin in a forest in the English Lake District. Win has been talking excitedly about this break for months – it's ages since we've been away. So far so good. But, unfortunately, she spent the first night here as sick as she has been for years. She is sleeping peacefully now, but I have been battling away with some totally irrational and unfair thoughts as I wait for her to wake up: 'Why are you allowing this, Lord? You know how much we needed this break, and how much we have been looking forward to it!'

Entitlement is raising its ugly head again! To add insult to injury, the forecasters have reported that Storm Gareth is on its way, so we know the sort of weather to expect for the next few days: winds of up to 75 miles an hour and almost continual rain – oh joy!

Memory 'loss'

How easily I allow all my experience of God's goodness, faithfulness and provision to be wiped clean from my mind by temporary disappointments or setbacks.

It was exactly that way with the children of Israel (see pages 37–38). When the twelve spies returned to the Israelite camp from reconnoitring the land of Canaan, the people chose to believe the negative report of the ten and to ignore the positive report of the two. Immediately, they saw the situation in Canaan as a huge setback. It was not yet a setback, of course, it just had the potential for significant problems. Nevertheless, it was enough to nullify for them all God's faithfulness since he had rescued them so dramatically from their captivity in Egypt: 'You grumbled in your tents and said, "The LORD hates us; so he brought us out of Egypt to deliver us into the hands of the Amorites to destroy us"' (Deuteronomy 1:27). After all their experience of God's deliverance and provision, it was remarkable how they forgot everything and concluded that the Lord hated them and wanted to destroy them.

> *'The deliberate engagement of*
> *the mind in times of difficulty and*
> *disappointment is key to living*
> *a life of gratitude.'*

Memory is so crucial to thanksgiving; the deliberate engagement of the mind in times of difficulty and disappointment is key to living a life of gratitude. As I sit here in the Lake District feeling a bit glum, with the wind howling and the rain pouring, waiting to see how Win is when she wakes up, I need to look back and remember – *intentionally.* As I do so, I see that if God had dealt fairly with me, I would have been destroyed long ago, for my true story is one of outrageous grace.

Time out

I have found that I must build into my daily and weekly routines vital spaces in which to remember. Unless I control my life today, it would move at such a frenetic pace that I would continually plan the next thing, leaving no time to reflect on the last thing. There would be no enjoyment of this moment because the next moment is uppermost in my mind. With my activist nature, I am often guilty of this. I am up in the morning, planning the day, working out schedules and writing lists of what I want to achieve before the end of it.

It used to be that way with my visits to the gym. I had worked it out to the minute: five minutes from my office to the gym, a forty-five-minute workout, a quick shower and then an apple on the way back to the office. Lunch and gym could all be done within the hour! I couldn't understand how other people found time to relax in the steam room. Eventually, my gym visits extended to a minimum of seventy-five minutes and I joined the guys in the steam room. Fifteen minutes in the middle of the day was an excellent space in which to catch my breath to reflect. I would often come away spiritually and physically refreshed because I had stopped to reflect on God and his goodness to me.

We don't need to 'find time' for a breathing space, for the time is already there. We need to *take* time – grab time – to make it a habit of our lives to carve out those important periods in our days. To do so is particularly vital in seasons of difficulty and pressure. In certain sports, when things are not going well for the team, 'time out' can be called: just a brief pause for the team to catch its breath and remember the coach's instructions before getting back into the game.

As we face difficulties in our lives, we can be sure that Satan will be intent on using them to bring us down. We must learn to pause and take that time out, reminding ourselves of all that we know of God through his Word and our experience with him down through the years. We need to use that space to reassure ourselves that God is with us through the indwelling Holy Spirit.

Good times and lurking dangers

It is not just the tough times that are particularly dangerous. The easier and apparently successful times in our lives can be even more perilous.

Moses gave this solemn warning to the children of Israel as they prepared to enter the Promised Land:

Observe the commands of the LORD your God, walking in his ways and revering him. For the LORD your God is bringing you into a good land – a land with streams and pools of water, with springs flowing in the valleys and hills; a land with wheat and barley, vines and fig-trees, pomegranates, olive oil and honey; a land where bread will not be scarce and you will lack nothing; a land where the rocks are iron and you can dig copper out of the hills.

When you have eaten and are satisfied, praise the LORD your God for the good land he has given you. Be careful that you do not forget the LORD your God, failing to observe his commands, his laws and his decrees that I am giving you this day. Otherwise, when you eat and are satisfied, when you build fine houses and settle down, and when your herds and flocks grow

large and your silver and gold increase and all you have is multiplied, then your heart will become proud and you will forget the LORD your God, who brought you out of Egypt, out of the land of slavery. He led you through the vast and dreadful desert, that thirsty and waterless land, with its venomous snakes and scorpions. He brought you water out of hard rock. He gave you manna to eat in the desert, something your fathers had never known, to humble and to test you so that in the end it might go well with you. You may say to yourself, 'My power and the strength of my hands have produced this wealth for me.' But remember the LORD your God, for it is he who gives you the ability to produce wealth, and so confirms his covenant, which he swore to your forefathers, as it is today.
(Deuteronomy 8:6–18, NIV84)

In those long years in the barren desert, the people had no-one to turn to but God. Sadly, as we noted, they regularly turned to him only to grumble and complain. But they knew on whom they were dependent. Little else underlined this fact more clearly than the morning exercise of gathering the manna that God provided: the Israelites did nothing but collect it. Without God's provision, they knew they would be finished. Now, however, they were to enter a good land, a land that God wanted them to enjoy. So after utter dependence on God, they now had complete abundance. They were to praise the Lord for the good land, recognizing who had given it to them (verse 10). Nevertheless, they forget their God, becoming proud and self-sufficient (verse 14). The good land would turn out to be as much a test as the desert for the children of Israel.

In his Thanksgiving message in 1863, Abraham Lincoln said to the American people:

We have grown in numbers, wealth and power, as no other nation has ever grown. But we have forgotten God. We have forgotten the gracious hand which preserved us in peace, and multiplied and enriched and strengthened us; and we have vainly imagined, in the deceitfulness of our hearts, that all these blessings were produced by some superior wisdom and virtue of our own. Intoxicated with unbroken success, we have become too self-sufficient to feel the necessity of redeeming and preserving grace, too proud to pray to the God that made us![2]

In times of success and prosperity we have a choice: we can thank God, recognizing our utter dependence on him, or we can forget him – forget that it is all down to his grace – and see ourselves as self-made successes.

Are there any secrets to getting our response right in times of both prosperity and adversity – and, indeed, always?

Rhythms of remembering

One thing I have found particularly helpful is to develop rhythms of remembering. Let me give you an example. Sometimes, for a season in my life, I will practise praise and prayer morning, noon and evening, enjoying focused time with God three times a day. Deliberately stopping and reflecting on God's goodness moves me away from focusing on myself, keeping God at, or restoring him to, the very centre of my life. I know that I live every moment in his presence but, personally, I need those focused times to recognize this reality, to remember, reflect, repent and renew my commitment.

I believe that Paul had in mind the fact that we live every moment in God's presence when he instructed the Thessalonian believers to 'pray continually' (1 Thessalonians 5:17). I think he was calling for an attitude of continual dependence. If we cultivate the understanding that we are weak but with him we are strong, then surely that continual sense of dependence on One so great and so dependable will lead to a life of thankfulness.

Sabbath

How, may I ask, is your sabbath discipline?

The sabbath principle gives regular time for a change of pace, a time to reflect on our own and, with our brothers and sisters during worship and praise, for remembering all that we have in Christ and receive from his good hand. Jesus called us to this regular remembrance. He chose a day to introduce a meal through which we could remember him and his great love for us. On the first day of the Feast of Unleavened Bread, the Jews sacrificed the Passover lamb. It was their moment to remember the day in their history when the angel of death had passed by their homes and had delivered them from bondage by bringing judgment on their Egyptian oppressors. Jesus chose that day of grateful remembrance in Israel to introduce a meal of remembrance for us:

When the hour came, Jesus and his apostles reclined at the table. And he said to them, 'I have eagerly desired to eat this Passover with you before I suffer. For I tell you, I will not eat it again until it finds fulfilment in the kingdom of God.'

After taking the cup, he gave thanks and said, 'Take this and divide it among you. For I tell you, I will not drink again from the fruit of the vine until the kingdom of God comes.'

And he took the bread, gave thanks and broke it, and gave it to them, saying, 'This is my body given for you; do this in remembrance of me.'
(Luke 22:14–19)

It must be very difficult to remember the Lord regularly in this way and not live a life of thanksgiving. How can we take the bread and wine and ever question God's love for us and his total commitment to us? That love and commitment are the solid basis of a life of thanksgiving on our part.

> *'How can we take the bread and wine
> and ever question God's love for us
> and his total commitment to us?'*

With such a solid basis, thankfulness becomes the choice that we make. As I wrote on page 45, we are not prisoners of our emotions or our circumstances. I wasted a month in Spain grumbling about my circumstances before I took 'time out'. Surely, it is wise for me to remember that experience and learn from it – learn that I shouldn't waste another moment feeling hard done by. Rather, I choose to look back and see faithfulness, love and commitment. I know that God, who has been with me in the past, is with me now and will be with me for ever;

the experiences of the past give certainty both for the present and the future.

Remember, remember

I think that David might well have been struggling the morning he woke up and wrote Psalm 103 (which we looked at on page 22). Were there challenging meetings ahead with his colleagues as he sought to lead the people? Was he battling with family issues? He speaks to himself: 'Praise the LORD O my soul; all my inmost being, praise his holy name. Praise the LORD, O my soul, and forget not all his benefits' (verses 1–2, NIV84). He does not allow his emotions to rule; he does not slip into despair without a struggle. He demands the commitment of all his faculties to give to God the praise and thanks that he deserves. He also urges himself to do two things: to praise God's holy name and not to forget all his benefits or blessings. There might have been many uncertainties before him, so he wanted to concentrate on the unchangeable certainties. Praising the name of God means praising his character.

While struggling in Spain all those years ago, I had some decisions to make and some actions to take. As we saw, I went to a quiet place and I used my will, my eyes, my voice and my memory; I started speaking to myself, reminding myself through song and through Scripture of the goodness of God. As I allowed the Word of Christ to dwell within me, the joy of Christ began to fill my heart again. For those of us seeking to walk with God, speaking to ourselves is certainly not the first sign of madness.

I want to close this chapter with a memorable example of 'time out'. I have already alluded to the fact that, for me, leading Christian organizations hasn't always been a walk in the park. Many years ago, a huge issue arose in one of them. As I sought to address it, I found that I was suddenly the centre of criticism. The issue was not easily resolved and, indeed, it raged for several months. During those months, I was up early in my study, asking God to deal with the problem and to deal with me as I attempted to resolve it.

Sometimes I felt exhausted and wondered if I should even continue in leadership. Praising the character of God during those months was a huge help. I also spent many hours in the Psalms, in which there were numerous reminders of the strength and faithfulness of God. At times, I felt hard done by, so being reminded of the justice of God was a real encouragement. When I felt that I was not dealing with the issue well, reminders of the mercy of God brought peace.

How crucial it is, particularly in times of uncertainty, to take time out to stand on certainties, and there is no greater certainty than the unchanging character of God. It was so easy during those difficult days for my whole attention to be on the problem before me. It was vital that I did not forget all God's benefits and blessings. These were those unchanging gifts from God, which no circumstances could ever steal from me.

Reflection

Read Psalm 77.

Asaph, whom we met in the study at the end of chapter 1, was struggling to the degree that he almost gave up the faith. He is struggling again here in Psalm 77. We can't be sure of the reason, but it is clearly serious. He is concerned that God might have rejected him and that this rejection might be permanent.

1 He is worried that he will never experience the Lord's favour again (verses 7–8).
2 Note how honest Asaph is in speaking to God (verse 9).
3 See how persistent he is (verses 1–2).
4 See how important memory is in bringing Asaph through his struggles. What, in particular, does he remember?

7

Gratitude, success and riches: the good, the bad and the ugly

My eldest granddaughter is studying physiotherapy at university, so I am under pressure these days. 'Don't cross your legs when you sit reading in the evening!' she instructs, when she spends time with Win and me. Oh dear! Even as I type these words into my PC, I realize that my legs are firmly crossed. It's hard to change the habits of a lifetime. My daughter-in-law has just spent a weekend at a course about physical posture as she tries to find an answer to a frustrating, nagging injury that has, for many months, kept her from the exercise she loves.

For our overall health, however, we need more than excellent physical posture. Our psychological posture is crucially important too. Professor Glynn Harrison explains, 'Like physical posture, our psychological posture (or mindset) is the way we incline towards the world. It determines what we see and how we see it.'[1] As we seek to cultivate a habit of gratitude, our psychological posture will have a huge impact on how we see the world.

The greatest benefit of gratitude is that it leads us away from self-absorption to God-centredness. As we reflect on the good things in our lives, we will continually be drawn back to the Giver of those good gifts. But Satan hates any praise of God. He makes sure that our fallen nature is prone to praise ourselves for the good things in our lives and to blame others, which may even include God, for the things that go wrong.

Reactions to riches

Jesus told the story of the rich farmer (Luke 12:13–21), who had clearly been significantly successful but gave absolutely no recognition to God for his success. No doubt he thought that his wise decisions were the reasons for his wealth. A bit like Bart Simpson, his attitude to God seemed to be 'thanks for nothing'; this is all down to me, to my hard work and great decision-making. But were the sun and the rain due to him? How was it that the quality of his soil was so good? No doubt if a storm had wrecked his crop, God would have been blamed. He was rich but, as Jesus says, not 'towards God'.

King David's attitude could not have been more different. He is offering, and encouraging others to offer, gifts for the building of the temple. This temple was not to be a building for humans but for the Lord God (1 Chronicles 29:1), so only the very best would do. It was a fabulously successful fund-raising campaign. David gave from the wealth of the nation (verse 2) and from his own personal riches (verses 3–5). Then the leaders in the nation consecrated themselves to the Lord and became part of this hugely successful campaign. Imagine a newspaper headline at the time: 'Due to the amazing generosity of our king and the leaders of our nation, the building of the temple is now guaranteed.'

David did joyfully acknowledge the human factor in this successful initiative and the people acknowledged it too (verse 9); it is important to recognize and celebrate human achievements. But David recognized the unseen – that everything he and his people had, everything they gave, came from God, who was to be praised: 'But who am I, and who are my people, that we should be able to give as generously as this? Everything comes from you, and we give you only what comes from your hand' (verse 14). David also saw that even the desire to give in this way came from God, and that it was a privilege. His prayer was that the desire to give thankfully and joyfully to God would be sustained (verse 18).

David set the example of giving; the leaders of the community followed his example; and the people rejoiced and were grateful for what was achieved. The result was joy (verse 9) and the praising of God (verses 10 and 20). Their thankfulness, while recognizing the great achievement, turned their hearts to God and away from themselves. Spiritual health in their nation resulted from their giving and their gratitude.

Gratitude is good for us!

Gratitude and idolatry

Yet even here, because of the subtlety of our enemy Satan, we must be careful.

Jonathan Edwards was a great preacher, pastor, theologian and philosopher. His life was comparatively short, just 54 years long, but what an impact he had on the church, both in his time and today through his extensive writings. One of the subjects that he addressed was gratitude. In *The Religious Affections*, he wrote:

There is a certain gratitude that is a mere natural thing. Gratitude is one of the affections of the soul of man, as well as anger, and there is a gratitude that arises from self-love, very much in the same manner as anger does.[2]

He refers in this context to Saul, who was overcome with gratitude towards David for sparing his life and yet remained his habitual enemy. Edwards argues that when 'we have affections towards God, only or primarily for benefits we have received, our affection is only the exercise of natural gratitude'. He then goes on to write about what he refers to as gracious gratitude, which 'greatly differs from all that gratitude which natural men [and women] experience'.[3] Gracious gratitude is thankfulness for God himself, for who he is. Edwards adds:

> In a gracious gratitude, men are affected with the attribute of God's goodness and free grace not only as they are concerned in it, or as it affects their interest, but as part of the glory and beauty of God.[4]

John Piper writes:

> God is not glorified if the foundation of our gratitude is the worth of the gift and not the excellency of the Giver. If gratitude is not rooted in the beauty of God before the gift, it is probably disguised idolatry. May God grant us a heart to delight in him for who he is, so that all our gratitude for his gifts will be the echo of our joy in the excellency of the Giver.[5]

Simon the sorcerer is a clear example of 'disguised idolatry'. He was desperate to receive the gifts of God, yet had no thought of 'the excellency of the Giver'. He had been the centre of attention in the community as he mesmerized people with his magic (Acts 8:11). He had had a remarkable impact: 'All the people, both high and low, gave him their attention and exclaimed, "This man is the divine power known as the Great Power"' (verse 10, NIV84). Simon's message was all about Simon! 'He boasted that he was someone great' (verse 9). Then Philip the evangelist arrived in town with a very different message. 'He proclaimed the good news of the kingdom of God and the name of Jesus Christ' (verse 12). There was such a response that Luke records, 'the apostles in Jerusalem heard that Samaria had accepted the word of God' (verse 14). Simon himself professed belief and was baptized. He lost his position of prominence and wanted it back. He was convinced that if he could perform the great miracles that he saw accompanying Philip's ministry, his fame would return. He wanted that ability so badly that he was willing to pay because, no doubt, he had made a lot of money from his former fame and power in the region.

When Simon saw that the Spirit was given through the laying on of the apostles' hands, he offered them money and said, 'Give me also this ability so that everyone on whom I lay my hands may receive the Holy Spirit.' (Acts 8:19)

Simon would have been grateful for the gifts from God, but would there have been any recognition of or praise to the Giver?

Thanksgiving is an act of worship, turning us away from ourselves and fixing our hearts on God. In Hebrews 12:28, the writer, focusing on the fact that an eternal kingdom awaits us, shows this progression from thanks to praise: 'Therefore, since we are receiving a kingdom that cannot be shaken, let us be thankful, and so worship God acceptably with reverence and awe.'

C. S. Lewis wrote, 'A proud man is always looking down on things and people; and, of course, as long as you are looking down, you cannot see something that is above you.'[6] Thanksgiving draws us to God, giving him praise. Pride does the very opposite, leading to self-absorption. There is no room for God if we are full of ourselves. Pride leads to autonomy, to a self-made attitude that results in no need for God and no reason to be grateful to him.

Riches, success and ruin

We looked at David in the Old Testament, a king who, in the moment of great success, recognizes his dependence on God. Rather than becoming absorbed in his own achievements, he gives praise where it is due.

Belshazzar was a very different king. He was having the time of his life, enjoying a huge banquet with thousands of his nobles to celebrate his success. A high point arrived when he gave orders for the gold and silver goblets that his father (or, possibly, grandfather) Nebuchadnezzar had taken from the temple in Jerusalem to be brought to the party. The wine would be even more enjoyable when drunk from these symbols of a people defeated by Babylonian supremacy. Belshazzar was clearly revelling in the greatness of his dynasty and taking the opportunity publicly to despise the God of Israel. His success, he was convinced, showed where true power lay. But the revelries were brought to an abrupt end. The fingers of a human hand appeared and wrote on the plaster of the palace wall. Belshazzar became a physical wreck: his face turned pale, his knees knocked and his legs gave way (Daniel 5:1–6).

Daniel was called for. He had interpreted disturbing dreams during the reign of Belshazzar's father Nebuchadnezzar, making clear that the source of his wisdom was the God of Israel. Daniel's interpretation of and commentary on the writing – which no-one else could read, including all Belshazzar's enchanters, astrologers and diviners – didn't make for easy listening. He reminded Belshazzar that it was God who had given his father 'sovereignty and greatness and glory and splendour' (verse 18). 'But when his heart became arrogant and hardened with pride, he was deposed from his royal throne and stripped of his glory' (verse 20).

Belshazzar's arrogance certainly equalled his predecessor's. Daniel says:

You have set yourself up against the Lord of heaven. You had the goblets from his temple brought to you, and you and your nobles, your wives and your concubines drank wine from them. You praised the gods of silver and gold, of bronze, iron, wood and stone, which cannot see or hear or understand. But you did not honour the God who holds in his hand your life and all your ways. (Daniel 5:23–24)

As Daniel had interpreted Nebuchadnezzar's dream, the latter had a moment of understanding: 'The king said to Daniel, "Surely your God is the God of gods and the Lord of kings and a revealer of mysteries, for you were able to reveal this mystery"' (Daniel 2:47). But it didn't last long. Soon he had commissioned a huge image of gold to be made and was demanding that his subjects worship it. Those who refused were to be thrown into a blazing furnace (Daniel 3:1–6).

If only Nebuchadnezzar and Belshazzar had stopped and thought for a moment, they would have recalled that, in their moments of great crisis, it was to the God of Israel they had to turn. They would have remembered to whom they should have been grateful; it would have saved them from the desperate pride and arrogance that led to their tragic downfall. Self-absorption is destructive. 'Pride comes before a fall' is a proven truth, not merely a saying. Henry Smith wrote, 'Pride thrust proud Nebuchadnezzar out of men's society, proud Saul out of his kingdom, proud Adam out of paradise, proud Haman out of court and proud Lucifer out of heaven.'[7]

As we know by now, gratitude draws us to God to give him praise; it is a vital element of having our fallen attitude recalibrated to God-centred thinking. While achievements such as the building of the temple are to be recognized and celebrated, if we see these as simply resulting from our own ability and energy, pride settles in and self-absorption rules the day.

'I will ascend' ingrained

At the beginning of the chapter, I mentioned how difficult it is to change the habit of a lifetime. For me, a simple thing such as crossing my legs when sitting down is hard to unlearn. It's the first thing I do when I sit down because I have been doing it for so long. I get frustrated with myself because the habit is taking ages to discard. Well, the habit of self-absorption is an ancient problem and it's hard to shift too.

We saw in chapter 4 that the tyranny of pride began with Satan:

How have you fallen from heaven,
   morning star, son of the dawn!

You have been cast down to the earth,
  you who once laid low the nations!
You said in your heart,
  'I will ascend to the heavens;
I will raise my throne
  above the stars of God;
I will sit enthroned on the mount of assembly,
  on the utmost heights of Mount Zaphon.
I will ascend above the tops of the clouds;
  I will make myself like the Most High.'
But you are brought down to the realm of the dead,
  to the depths of the pit.
(Isaiah 14:12–15)

'I will ascend' is the cry of the proud heart. Satan was planning a pretty steep ascent – 'above the stars of God' no less. Was there any sign of thankfulness here for his already exalted position? No, it was not enough for him: 'I will ascend into heaven; I will raise my throne above the stars of God.' It's a clear formula. Pride destroys thanksgiving and where there is no thanksgiving, there is no spiritual health; there is no true worship, only idolatry.

'He humbled himself'

Pride began with Satan and it continues today. The daily battle with pride goes on in my life. Recently, a colleague was telling me with obvious joy of some success that he had seen in his ministry. I had to constrain myself, realizing that I could hardly wait for him to finish so that I could tell him a story from my own ministry of a comparable, or preferably greater, success than his! It's a struggle every day and I'm convinced that if I'm going to know any victory, I will need to focus on a person and a place. I will need to have the attitude of Jesus,

> who, being in very nature God,
>   did not consider equality with God something
>   to be grasped,
> but made himself nothing,
>   taking the very nature of a servant,
>   being made in human likeness.
> And being found in appearance as a man,
>   he humbled himself
>   and became obedient to death – even death
>   on a cross!
> (Philippians 2:6–8, NIV84)

This attitude of total humility draws Jesus to his Father: 'Therefore God exalted him to the highest place and gave him the name that is above every name' (verse 9, NIV84).

> *'It is at the cross that I find*
> *the great antidote to any foolish pride.'*

The cross is where I need to be. It is at the cross that I find the great antidote to any foolish pride. Here, I see myself truly, as Jesus bears my sin and curse and pays the debt that I could never pay. Here, I can have no inflated views of myself, for I am cut down to size. I see that, without Christ, I am nothing and, without his sacrifice, forever lost. If I can learn to live in the shadow of the cross, then a habit of thankfulness will be sure to result. And that habit of thankfulness is a key to our spiritual and emotional health.

Reflection

Read Psalm 27.

1 David was clearly in trouble when he wrote this psalm (verse 3). Where was his confidence as he faced this trouble (verses 1, 2 and 3)?
2 What was his one desire (verse 4)?
3 Can you see three reasons why David wanted to 'dwell in the house of the Lord' (verses 4–5)?
4 Sometimes, when we are under pressure, we want to take matters into our own hands. What was David's desire (verse 11)?

8

Gratitude and sovereignty

Be thankful his majesty is your protection, his glory is
your motivation, his grace is your help, and his wisdom
is your direction. He is infinitely smarter than you and
me in our most brilliant moments.[1]

The overnight flight to Manila seemed particularly long. I was
flying out to visit several hospitals treating the victims of a
terrorist attack on the crew of our Operation Mobilisation
ship MV *Doulos*. Terrorists had thrown grenades at a concert
being held beside the ship. Two people had been confirmed
dead and many were injured, some severely. It was one night
when I did not sleep: how could I minister effectively to the
injured, and what was I to say to the ship's company at their
morning devotions?

Sleep and sovereignty

Although this was certainly the most extreme event that
occurred while I was International Director of OM, there was
a continual stream of issues that had the potential to keep me
awake at night. Our ministry spanned more than a hundred
countries, some of them difficult places in which to serve
Christ. Along with all the terrific blessings of leading the
ministry, there were problems concerning people, money
shortages, security concerns and disunity, and many others –
I could add a great deal more to the list.

I am so grateful that early in my period of leadership, I had a very real sense of God saying, 'This is my work. You are to make your contribution, but it is my work.' I would go to bed with things spinning round in my head, nevertheless I often rested in the knowledge that the work was the Lord's and I was often able to put things down, even if it took some time to do so. I would say, 'Lord, it's yours. I have done my best today and I will do my best when I wake in the morning. Give me rest now, knowing that the work is in your sovereign hands.' Even so, there were sleepless nights; that overnight flight to Manila was certainly one of them, but they were surprisingly few as I increasingly learned to rest in the amazing, reassuring truth of God's sovereignty.

Not only will a life of thanksgiving liberate us from self-absorption, it will liberate us from worry and fear. 'Fear not' was the constant encouragement of Jesus when he was on earth. God is sovereign, for which I am so thankful. Sometimes, I confess, I still live as though I am in control of my affairs; if that were the case, it would give me every reason to fear! But it is not, for a sovereign God has his hands on the reins of the universe and of my life, and he does not allow those reins to slip out of his hands.

'God has his hands on the reins of the universe and of my life, and he does not allow those reins to slip out of his hands.'

Persecution and sovereignty

Peter and John were going up to the temple to share in the daily afternoon prayer service. At the same time, a man who had been crippled from birth was being carried there, as happened every day, to sit and beg for his livelihood. He asked Peter and John for a contribution, but he got a lot more than he asked for!

> Peter looked straight at him, as did John. Then Peter said, 'Look at us!' So the man gave them his attention, expecting to get something from them.
> Then Peter said, 'Silver or gold I do not have, but what I do have I give to you. In the name of Jesus Christ of Nazareth, walk.' Taking him by the right hand, he helped him up, and instantly the man's feet and ankles became strong. He jumped to his feet and began to walk.
> (Acts 3:4–8)

You can imagine what a scene this caused. The man had been something of a fixture at the temple, the public passing him every day as they went up to worship. Now he was walking and jumping and praising God (verse 9). All the people ran to the scene 'filled with wonder and amazement' (verses 10–11). The response of the crowd gave Peter an opportunity for a sermon, which he certainly grabbed with both hands (verses 12–26).

The Sadducees (a Jewish sect) did not appreciate this turn of events. They were a very influential group who denied any teaching that was not clearly supported by the books of Moses: Genesis to Deuteronomy. In particular, they denied life after death in any form. It was the fact that Peter and John had preached 'in Jesus the resurrection of the dead' that really upset them (Acts 4:2). They seized the two men and had them imprisoned overnight. The next morning, a hearing held by the council of Jewish religious leaders gave the irrepressible Peter another opportunity for a brief sermon (Acts 4:8–12).

The situation for the religious leaders was difficult because the crippled man who had been healed was present at the hearing (verse 14) and 'all the people were praising God for what had happened' (verse 21). Eventually, they let Peter and John go with a warning 'not to speak or teach at all in the name of Jesus' (verse 18). This moment was very significant for the early church: it was the beginning of its long history of persecution.

The response of Peter and John was to return to the community and report all that had happened to them: 'When [the community] heard this, they raised their voices together in prayer to God. "Sovereign Lord," they said, "you made the heavens and the earth and the sea, and everything in them"' (verse 24). They immediately recognized that, in this crisis, it was the sovereign Lord of the universe to whom they must turn. They knew that in the Old Testament God had spoken of this opposition; he was certainly not surprised by it. Even the religious leaders' earlier conspiracy against Jesus was only what God's 'power and will had decided beforehand should happen' (verse 28). The first Christian creed was probably the shortest: 'Jesus is Lord.' He is the ultimate Sovereign and Ruler. You can imagine what that profound understanding meant to those early believers as they faced persecution and were scattered around the world, losing many of their leaders to martyrdom. It is this conviction that should rule our lives and calm our fears today.

By resting in the sovereignty of God at this time of crisis, the early church was following in the footsteps of its Master. In a life-or-death moment, the trust of Jesus in the sovereign rule of his Father is clear. He stands in front of Pilate, who says to him, 'Don't you realise I have power either to free you or to crucify you?' (John 19:10). And that is how it must have appeared: Pilate represented the most powerful man on earth, the Roman emperor Tiberius Caesar. 'Jesus answered, "You would have no power over me if it were not given to you from above"' (verse 11). Jesus is conscious of a far greater authority than that of Rome or Caiaphas or the Jewish mob; he knows his future is in his Father's hands. The authority Pilate wields is a temporary gift given to him by God. Our God is sovereign over all; an earthly governor can act only with his permission (Romans 13:1).

The world's worries and God's sovereignty

With such a conviction, Jesus could teach his disciples the following:

Therefore I tell you, do not worry about your life, what you will eat or drink; or about your body, what you will wear. Is not life more than food, and the body more than clothes? Look at the birds of the air; they do not sow or reap or store away in barns, and yet your heavenly Father feeds them. Are you not much more valuable than they? Can any one of you by worrying add a single hour to your life?

And why do you worry about clothes? See how the flowers of the field grow. They do not labour or spin. Yet I tell you that not even Solomon in all his splendour was dressed like one of these. If that is how God clothes the grass of the field, which is here today and tomorrow is thrown into the fire, will he not much more clothe you –

you of little faith? So do not worry, saying, 'What shall we eat?' or 'What shall we drink?' or 'What shall we wear?' For the pagans run after all these things, and your heavenly Father knows that you need them. But seek first his kingdom and his righteousness, and all these things will be given to you as well. Therefore do not worry about tomorrow, for tomorrow will worry about itself. Each day has enough trouble of its own. (Matthew 6:25–34)

We celebrate that a sovereign God, who is our Father, is in control of his world and of our lives. This means that both our ambitions and our anxieties should be completely different from those of the people around us. Watch an advertisement break on television and you will see what concerns and preoccupies so many. It is just what Jesus said: food, drink and clothing – 'What shall we eat? What shall we drink? What shall we wear?' (verse 31) – and, of course, the driving concern to do everything possible to extend the length of our lives (verse 27). Jesus says, 'The pagans run after all these things' (verse 32), things which should not be the primary concerns of God's people. In *The Message*, Eugene Peterson paraphrases it like this: 'People who don't know God and the way he works fuss over these things, but you know God and how he works.' We should be different because God is our heavenly Father, and we know him and how he works.

Our age of entitlement leads to anxiety: if I am not experiencing good health, financial stability and social well-being, then I panic. Such worries would be understandable if the final responsibility for them were to lie with us. In all of them, we have a vital part to play, but we take the necessary steps under the eye of a sovereign God, who is our Father and, according to Jesus, knows our needs even before we mention them to him.

A strong track record

The sovereign God, whom we choose to trust, has a strong track record. We have seen that he provided daily manna for his people as they wandered in the wilderness. Every morning, it was there, with a double portion for the sabbath on the sixth day, every week. The people for whom he provided this bounty were not grateful but grumbling (Numbers 11:6). The day after they began to eat the food of the Promised Land, the manna supply ceased (Joshua 5:12). At God's command, Aaron placed a portion of the last manna in a jar. It was to be kept as a testimony to future generations of God's provision for his people (Exodus 16:33–34). Through his servants the ravens, God brought bread and meat to his faithful prophet Elijah, who had given Ahab, the king of Israel, a prophecy from the Lord and was now hiding from him (1 Kings 17:6). Later, after Elijah had fled from Jezebel, Ahab's wife, God provided fresh bread and a jar of water and he refused to answer Elijah's suicidal prayer request to die (1 Kings 19:3–6). The apostle Paul in the New Testament was convinced that 'God will meet all your needs according to the riches of his glory in Christ Jesus' (Philippians 4:19).

Do you have an equivalent of Aaron's jar of testimony? I do. Several years ago, I was invited to speak at a family convention organized by the churches of Khartoum in Sudan. The meetings were huge, and I had never before experienced anything like the culture of those meetings; there were healings, and the casting out of demons was an expected element in each one. This was a bit different from normal life in my home church and from most of the meetings I had addressed around the world. To say I felt totally inadequate would be an understatement and yet, in amazing ways over the eight days of meetings, I saw the faithfulness and sufficiency of God. I have a 'walking stick of testimony' from that event. A woman was brought into the meetings; she was unable to walk and was supported by her family. At the end of the service, she came to the front, threw her stick on to the stage and walked away. I brought her walking stick home with me. It is in my office as a reminder of God's faithfulness and his sufficiency despite my inadequacy. Now, we know that God doesn't always work in this particular way, but we praise him when he does.

Are we going to live lives of grateful trust in God's fatherly care or of constant worry, thinking ourselves to be in control of those things which God is committed to look after?

Carefree, not careless

Trusting in God is not a licence for lethargy. We aren't to think that we can sit back in idleness because God is in control and he will provide. If that is how we respond, it is clear, to use Peterson's paraphrase, that we 'don't know God or how he works'. The ant comes to mind: 'It stores its provisions in summer and gathers its food at harvest' (Proverbs 6:8). The writer of Proverbs gives that example to challenge the lifestyle of someone he refers to as a 'sluggard' – a lazy, foolish individual (verse 6).

We have a responsibility to work hard to put food on the table and to look after our bodies, but we can also be carefree rather than careless if the kingdom is first in our lives. If we are unduly preoccupied with food, our bodies and so on, how can we 'seek first his kingdom and his righteousness'? But if the kingdom has priority in our lives, then 'all these things will be given to [us] as well' (Matthew 6:33). That is the context in which the passage in Matthew 6 must be understood. Jesus has just challenged his hearers about what they treasure, where they fix their eyes and who or what masters their lives (verses 19–24). Once we have our priorities correct, we do not need to worry about our lives (verse 25). What an example Jesus is in the wilderness as he faces the most intense of temptations! The devil seeks to trip him up on 'life' issues: food, fame and future. But his eye is firmly fixed on his Father: 'It is written: "Worship the Lord your God, and serve him only"' (Matthew 4:10).

Gratitude can become a way of life. As our trust in a sovereign God and our submission to him grow, our worries decrease. God our Father is unchanging; it therefore follows that he must be faithful. If he were ever to be unfaithful, he would change. His covenant promises and his complete faithfulness rest on the foundation of his unchanging nature. If you are struggling with anxiety, insecurity or discouragement, meditate on these certainties. God will always be true to his word; his lovingkindness and faithfulness never fail. Allow gratitude for who he is and the fact that he is yours – your Father – to flood your heart and wash away the discouragements.

Gratitude must become much more than our response to acts of kindness. If we recognize that we live under the care of our sovereign God and Father, who always has our best interests at heart, then the anxiety of epidemic proportions in our society will be challenged by a people whose peace and gratitude are grounded in knowing who is in ultimate control.

Reflection

Read Psalm 2.

Note that 'his anointed' (verse 2) refers finally to the Lord Jesus Christ. See Acts 13:26, in which Paul confirms the fulfilment of this prophecy, when the rulers failed to recognize the Son, the Anointed One.

1 What is the plan of the world's leaders?
2 What is God's response to their plans?
3 Who will be victorious? Note the tense of the verb in verse 4.
4 What should have been the response of the leaders to the overwhelming sovereign power of God? Note 'kiss' (verse 12), which speaks of homage and submission.
5 This sovereign God is our Father. How do you feel about living under his daily care?

9

Learning and contentment

Contentment makes poor men rich; discontent makes rich men poor.[1]

When I was working with Operation Mobilisation, Win and I rarely enjoyed a leisurely breakfast together. Today, in a different season of our lives, that is happily very different. Yet those breakfasts often reveal one of my great weaknesses. It's a weakness that you might remember from page 55. After I've asked Win what her day holds, it's not long before I am putting together a schedule – I would fill every minute of every day, if I could! I love drawing up 'to do' lists, and find it very satisfying to tick off the tasks accomplished as the day progresses. Fortunately, Win has learned to live with my being so driven.

What is the balance between being disciplined and being driven? I am just not *content* if I am not achieving something. Taken to an extreme, this can be harmful. My prayer life can become dominated by requests for God's help to get things done. The exercise of prayer becomes another opportunity to make lists and easily deteriorates into another box-ticking exercise. I don't enjoy God in that moment because my mind is focused on what I need to achieve later on. Not only is there no enjoyment of God today because I am planning tomorrow but also neither is there next week, next month, next . . . You get the picture.

The Lord tells us to 'Be still and know that I am God' (Psalm 46:10). But I don't want to be still – I want to be on the move, doing and completing stuff. I might briefly express my gratitude to God for his goodness and for all that I have in Christ because that's what Christians do. However, that is not where my heart is: praise and gratitude are squeezed out by the focus on me and what I need to achieve. Some days I look back and recognize that this driven attitude has stopped me spending quality time with my friends, my neighbours and even family members. I curtail our conversations because the priority is to tick off another job. My priorities become skewed.

How would I have survived if I had been given the clear calling and the amazing abilities of the apostle Paul? He was called to be an apostle to the Gentiles and yet was imprisoned. How could he ever get the job done, confined by the four walls of his cell? The New Testament book of Philippians is one of Paul's so-called 'prison letters' and it is where he makes his famous statement: 'I have learned the secret of being content in any and every situation' (Philippians 4:12). The specific context of that statement concerns his material needs. He is content if he has much or if he has little; when you read the letter, though, it is clear that, even in prison, with all its limitations, Paul recognizes the hand of God on his life. Although I am sure there were battles, his contentment is clear for us to see.

Let's review our terrain. The historian Arthur M. Schlesinger observes that 'with the acceleration in the rate of social change, humans become creatures characterized by inextinguishable discontent. Wishes are boundless, and therefore can never be fully satisfied.'[2] The continual drip, drip, drip of the message is that 'we need more and we deserve more' and, for a society based on ever-increasing production and consumption to continue, this message must win the day. What Paul wrote about contentment from his cell in Rome would make today's marketing professionals tremble.

We are endlessly encouraged to look for the next thing, the next experience that will surely satisfy: the next weekend, the next holiday, the next big purchase. After all, 'We're worth it!' The whole intention is to move us away from who we are and what we have, to who we want to be and what we believe we should have. The present is never enjoyed; we are frustrated because of what we don't have and envious of those who do have. Rodney Clapp writes, 'The consumer is schooled in insatiability . . . taught that people basically consist of unmet needs that can be appeased by goods and experiences.'[3] Somebody once said that the whole direction of our age is to spend money we don't have, to buy goods we don't need, to impress people we don't like! That may be a bit over the top, but isn't there some truth to it?

Be still

Contentment invites me to look at God and recognize that, regardless of what I have accumulated or how society might view me, I am accepted in Christ and adopted into God's family, which must be sufficient reason for continual gratitude. Gratitude frees me to live contentedly today; it does not compel me to focus anxiously on tomorrow or be tormented by yesterday.

Speaking personally, I began to deal with my driven nature when I built into my life periods of stillness and solitude. Thankfully, I have always been disciplined about having a daily quiet time – it is not difficult for driven people to be disciplined about such exercises. But, as I implied on page 89, even my quiet time can become a box-ticking exercise, something I want to achieve in a certain time-span. There are a certain number of chapters to read each day if I plan to go through the Bible in a year; there is a prayer list to be completed or a chapter to be finished if I'm using a devotional. Those times are important – I need them – but what I need more is time with no agenda other than being in my Father's presence, recognizing the privilege that I have, and deliberately recalling all the examples of his faithfulness and goodness to me since my last period of stillness.

A learning curve

On pages 36–37, we saw that both the fall of Lucifer and the fall of humanity had their origins in ingratitude. Satan was the marketing professional extraordinaire in the garden. Adam and Eve had everything they needed and more, but Satan encouraged Eve to question the goodness of God; that is what discontentment is – questioning the goodness of God. In the New Testament, Satan tried to use the same strategy with Jesus in the wilderness. He attempted to sow seeds of discontent about Jesus' heavenly Father's provision. When Satan failed, he sought to make Jesus desire recognition, position and power. These manipulative devices should not surprise us because we have already seen how Satan's own downfall was occasioned by discontentment. He was discontented with the position God had assigned him in the hierarchy of angelic beings (Isaiah 14:13–15). We are people born with the sinful nature of the discontented Adam and Eve, so we have to learn contentment – it doesn't come naturally. Although Paul explained to the Philippians that he was 'content whatever the circumstances', he also said that it was something he had to learn. I suspect that, compared with Paul, I would be considered laid-back rather than driven.

The traditional view of Moses' law is that there are 613 commandments that a faithful Jew must keep; Paul says that he scored 100 per cent; he tells us that 'as for legalistic righteousness, [he was] faultless' (Philippians 3:6, NIV84). It is hard to imagine the discipline and devotion that each day must have required. I wonder, though, did he go to bed at night a contented man? He writes, 'Sin, seizing the opportunity afforded by the commandment, produced in me every kind of covetous desire' (Romans 7:8, NIV84). So how did such a driven man learn contentment? Peace finally came not through his own efforts but through trusting in the finished work of Christ, and from receiving righteousness as a gift rather than spending a lifetime striving for it. Meet Paul at the end of his life, which must have consisted of a long, arduous learning curve, but his contentment is clear:

What is more, I consider everything a loss compared to the surpassing greatness of knowing Christ Jesus my Lord, for whose sake I have lost all things. I consider them rubbish, that I may gain Christ and be found in him not having a righteousness of my own that comes from the law, but that which is through faith in Christ – the righteousness that comes from God and is by faith. (Philippians 3:8–9, NIV84)

For I am already being poured out like a drink offering, and the time for my departure is near. I have fought the

good fight, I have finished the race, I have kept the faith. Now there is in store for me the crown of righteousness, which the Lord, the righteous Judge, will award to me on that day – and not only to me, but also to all who have longed for his appearing.
(2 Timothy 4:6–8)

A magnificent way to die: Paul looks backwards, forwards and within himself, and is content. Righteousness comes as a gift from God rather than through his intense efforts, which is the fundamental lesson he learns – there is no contentment without that understanding. But even with such a solid foundation of contentment in place, struggles will continue. Surely Paul had questions about his days in prison. The criticism that he received even from his brothers and sisters in Christ must have left him confused and sad. In Philippi, there were those who used their preaching to 'stir up trouble for [him] while [he was] in chains' (Philippians 1:17). Yet his remarkable response was 'But what does it matter? The important thing is that in every way, whether from false motives or true, Christ is preached. And because of this I rejoice' (verse 18).

For Paul, life was not all about him, his discomfort in prison or the injustice of his treatment by those who should have known much better. It was all about Christ and that was what counted. He recognized that his imprisonment was 'advancing the gospel' as it became clear to 'the whole palace guard and to everyone else that [he was] in chains for Christ' (verse 13). Contentment grew as he and others saw that he was put there 'for the defence of the gospel' (verse 16).

When the cause of Christ is our chief priority and we recognize a sovereign God, and that the glory of his Son is our Father's chief priority, then even in the most difficult circumstances we can learn contentment. A prison is preferable to a palace if we know it is where God wants us to be. We come to see that Christ is being made known through our difficulties.

'A prison is preferable to a palace
if we know it is where God wants us to be.'

Persevere!

It was not long after the day of Pentecost that persecution began, first of the apostles and then of the whole church: 'On that day a great persecution broke out against the church in Jerusalem, and all except the apostles were scattered throughout Judea and Samaria' (Acts 8:1). You can imagine the shock that might have caused the believers to say to themselves, 'I never realized that following Christ would lead to this!' As these first Christians struggled for shelter and food, they must have wondered what God was doing. Then, one day, they received a letter from their pastor, James the apostle and leader of the church in Jerusalem, which would have immediately revived memories of home. Tears of relief and expectation might have begun to flow – surely there would be sympathy and encouragement from their pastor?

James, a servant of God and of the Lord Jesus Christ,
To the twelve tribes scattered among the nations:
Greetings.
Consider it pure joy, my brothers and sisters, whenever you face trials of many kinds, because you know

that the testing of your faith produces perseverance. Let perseverance finish its work so that you may be mature and complete, not lacking anything.
(James 1:1–4)

James must have seemed insensitive. Shouldn't he have begun with words of comfort and understanding? But this letter reflects true encouragement. The apostle was assuring the believers that the trials they were enduring were not random. There was a divine and good purpose to them; if they responded well, then spiritual maturity would be the product. If they were able to recognize this, then joy, not doubt and disillusionment, would result.

If we know that there will be a positive outcome to our difficulties, we can know contentment as we endure them, which builds character. For example, imagine that I'm watching the semi-final of the soccer World Cup, in which England is playing Germany. Germany scores in the first half; the jubilant excitement of the German players and supporters leaves me depressed. To my utter astonishment, however, England scores twice in the second half and that is how the game ends. The next day I think, 'I enjoyed that match so much that I will watch it again on the catch-up service.' This time when Germany scores there is no depression. Indeed, it is replaced by a rather disgraceful smugness because I know the final result.

Take another example: a man sits watching a butterfly trying to force its way out of a cocoon. After a few hours of struggle, it doesn't seem to be making much progress. He decides to give it a helping hand. Taking his penknife, he cuts the end of the cocoon. The butterfly pops out, but its wings are far from fully developed: it will never fly. It needed the struggle to develop into a mature butterfly, ready for flight.

Often Christ is made known, and we develop our relationship with him, amid difficulty. But when we know the end result, contentment and gratitude can be our experience, even when we're still in the middle of the storm. It takes time to learn to live by these countercultural principles in a day when comfort and material success are the goals for so many. With the help of the Holy Spirit, however, it is possible. He will lead us to the cross because that is where the secret of contentment lies. There we see the righteousness of God, available to us because the righteous One died in our place. We know that Christ was exalted there, in all his pain, blood and suffering.

So how can I – a naturally driven person – learn to be content day by day? I need space, time for reflection and time to ask, 'What really matters? Is life all about me? Will I be satisfied at the end of the day if all the items on the list are ticked off or if Christ has been proclaimed, even if that means there are no ticks on the page? Will I take time to see the hand of God at work, even in and through the difficulties I might be grappling with?'

Contentment means safety for me. If I am always striving, wishing for more rather than grateful for all I have, living tomorrow rather than in the moment today, then remaining in God's peace will elude me.

Reflection

Read Psalm 23.

In this well-known psalm, we see the words of a very contented person. He lacks nothing in the present: his 'cup overflows' (verse 5). He has no fears about the future; even the valley of the shadow of death holds no fears. This can be our experience too, but only because the Lord Jesus experienced the very opposite.

1 Now read Psalm 22. It speaks very clearly of the Lord Jesus and the horrendous suffering he endured on our behalf. Here's the cost of being a 'good shepherd' (see John 10:11).
2 Take time now to thank and praise God for all that his Son has endured for you. Think again about the only rational response to such sacrificial love.

10

Gratitude as a weapon: fighting back in weakness

For the battle is not yours, but God's.
(2 Chronicles 20:15)

When I was invited to speak at the Maramon Convention in Kerala, southern India, I was told it was a big one. It certainly was! The number of people (particularly during the weekend of this week-long event) was reported to be between 100,000 and 150,000. Each year the Christians would build a huge covering from coconut palms to give some protection from the sun that blazes all day every day of the convention. From the covered platform, it seemed that there were people as far as the eye could see. Thankfully, the amplification was amazing.

I had been asked to speak at two of the main evening sessions. On my first evening, I was still a little jet-lagged. The churchmanship was something I was not used to: it appeared to be Orthodox in style. Everyone who participated had to kiss the bishop's ring as they went to the podium. My message had to be translated and I had met the translator only briefly the night before. I was totally out of my comfort zone, utterly weak and helpless.

But God, in his extraordinary grace, used me for his glory that evening. I went to my room with two things in my mind:

'God, that was all of you: you are to be glorified and how thankful I am.' I lay on my bed and spent some time expressing my thanks. That's what a sense of weakness does – it makes us give the glory to the one who deserves it and it draws thankfulness from our hearts.

An offensive weapon

Thankfulness can also be a weapon. As I walked through the blazing sun towards the podium from which I was to speak, I felt my utter weakness. However, I should also have been thanking God that what I was about to do would not be in my own strength but in his omnipotent power.

Jehoshaphat was a wonderful example of someone who used thankfulness as a weapon. In 2 Chronicles, we read of him and his people facing insurmountable odds as a huge multinational army marched against them. He said to God, 'We do not know what to do, but our eyes are on you' (2 Chronicles 20:12). His only hope was God and divine intervention, and he needed to know what God wanted him to do. He proclaimed a fast and the people willingly responded and came together to seek God (verses 2–4). Jehoshaphat stood before them and cried out to God. His prayer affirmed God's sovereign rule over all the kingdoms of the earth; he remembered God's faithfulness to the children of Israel throughout their history. He also made the commitment that, whatever happened, they would stand in God's presence before the temple that bore his name and would cry out to him in their distress (verse 9). He was convinced that God would hear their cry and save them (verses 5–9). The injustice of the situation troubled him: the nations arrayed against him were those that God had prevented Israel from invading when they had come out of Egypt. Jehoshaphat cried out for justice.

Confidence and weakness

So Jehoshaphat was confident; his confidence was based on his conviction of the greatness of God and on Israel's history with God, but still he sensed and vocalized his utter weakness: 'For we have no power to face this vast army that is attacking us' (verse 12). This is often the Christian experience: we are convinced of the greatness of God, assured by our experience with him over many years, yet we still face situations that leave us feeling completely weak.

In the New Testament, Paul often wrote of this sense of weakness. He struggled with what he described as his 'thorn in the flesh' (2 Corinthians 12:7). We don't know what the thorn was, but we do know that it gave him a sense of utter weakness. He pleaded with the Lord three times to take it away. But the Lord did not, choosing to leave his servant feeling weak. Instead, God explained an essential truth to him: 'My power is made perfect in weakness' (verse 9). The Lord also reassured Paul that there would be sufficient grace to deal with it. This revelation caused Paul to delight in his weakness rather than plead for its removal. He concluded with a statement that I still – after more than half a century of reading it and many times preaching it – find hard to believe in the heat of the battle: 'For when I am weak, then I am strong' (verse 10).

We return to Jehoshaphat, who cried out to the Lord, 'We do not know what to do' (2 Chronicles 20:12). God responded through the word of his prophet: 'Do not be afraid or dis-couraged . . . For the battle is not yours, but God's' (verse 16).

Confident in God, yet feeling utterly uncertain and completely weak, all Jehoshaphat could do was entrust himself and his people to God's mercy and power. The next morning, he sent his army out against the coalition troops. Leading the army forward were not archers or swordsmen but a choir, which sang 'Give thanks to the LORD, for his love endures for ever' (verse 21). If the battle is the Lord's and we know that we are in his arms and nothing can happen to us outside his loving control, we will lift our voices in praise of his love, which endures for ever, even in our nation's darkest moments.

Ambushing Satan with song

I love the title that John Piper gave to a message he preached on this passage in 1985: 'Ambushing Satan with Song'. The song was important. The people of Judah knew that the battle was the Lord's, but they did not sit at home waiting for victory to be announced. They took God at his word and went forwards, declaring their conviction in that word. It was 'as they began to sing and praise' (verse 22) that things began to happen. God wants us to know that our praise, thanks and song confuse and dishearten our enemies.

In chapter 5, I described my first missionary trip and how miserable I was for the first month. When I prayed and sang my thanks to God in that quiet place in Spain, it certainly lifted my spirits. But there was more to it than that. I have no doubt that I was under attack in those days, for Satan was not happy for me to learn the lessons that God wanted to teach me; he did not want my witness to be heard in that part of Spain, at a time when there was a minimal evangelical church presence. I firmly believe that the praise, songs and prayers were an offensive weapon against the enemy.

*'I firmly believe that the praise,
songs and prayers were an offensive
weapon against the enemy.'*

I have been there many times in my life, and I am sure every
follower of Christ has too. The battle is raging and you cannot
see a way through. You seem to be sinking; you have no
answers for the questions racing around your mind. You cry
out to God in your pain and confusion, but there seems to
be no reply. There is a principle and a pattern of factors here:
confidence in God's power, experience of human weakness,
reliance on God, recognition of his intervention, giving all
glory to him and thankfulness.

Return with me to the New Testament book of Acts. Paul
and his companions were going to a place of prayer. On the
way, they were met by a slave girl who was possessed by a
demonic spirit that enabled her to predict the future, which
earned a nice income for her owners. Her message was clear:
'These men are servants of the Most High God, who are telling
you the way to be saved' (Acts 16:17). John Stott asks, 'But why
should a demon engage in evangelism?' He suggests that 'the
ulterior motive was to discredit the gospel by associating it in
people's minds with the occult'.[1] The girl followed Paul and
his companions for many days, no doubt shrieking out this
claim. This troubled Paul and perhaps the desperate condition
of this slave girl troubled him as well. Finally, he was so uncomfortable that he commanded the spirit to come out of her
in the name of Jesus Christ. Immediately, the spirit left
her. Her owners were angry; they'd lost their meal ticket. But
they concealed the real, economic reason for their anger from
the magistrates. They cleverly presented their concerns as

political: 'These men are Jews, and are throwing our city into an uproar by advocating customs unlawful for us Romans to accept or practise' (verses 20–21). These accusations about introducing a religion that was not sanctioned by the state were serious.

The response was brutal:

The crowd joined in the attack against Paul and Silas, and the magistrates ordered them to be stripped and beaten. After they had been severely flogged, they were thrown into prison, and the jailer . . . put them in the inner cell and fastened their feet in the stocks.
(verses 22–24)

Bruised and lacerated in the inner cell (probably a very dark place), Paul and Silas prayed: the word used here indicates an attitude not of petition but of adoration and worship. They sang hymns to God, sufficiently loudly for the other prisoners to hear. It seemed that the devil had done his worst, so the only response was praise and worship.

Madame Guyon, who spent ten years of her life in French prisons, wrote this moving hymn during her confinement:

A little bird I am,
    Shut from the fields of air,
And in my cage, I sit and sing
    To Him who placed me there;
Well pleased a prisoner to be,
Because, my God, it pleaseth Thee.

Nought have I else to do,
    I sing the whole day long;

And He whom most I love to please,
  Doth listen to my song;
He caught and bound my wandering wing;
But still He bends to hear me sing.

Thou hast an ear to hear,
  A heart to love and bless;
And though my notes were e'er so rude,
  Thou wouldst not hear the less;
Because Thou knowest as they fall,
That love, sweet love, inspires them all.

My cage confines me round;
  Abroad I cannot fly;
But though my song is closely bound,
  My heart's at liberty.
My prison walls cannot control
The flight, the freedom of the soul.

O it is good to soar
  These bolts and bars above!
To Him whose purpose I adore,
  Whose providence I love;
And in Thy mighty will to find
The joy, the freedom of the mind.
(Jeanne Guyon, 1648–1717)[2]

The devil cannot stand against a song like this. It is a highly effective offensive weapon. And that proved to be the case as Paul and his companion sang their hearts out in the Philippian prison. As we saw in chapter 5, it led to the jailer and his household being converted and baptized, and joy and freedom reigning in their home.

It really is difficult to stop or silence truly grateful people. You just cannot keep them down, even if they are in stocks in the inner cell, smarting from their beatings. It is immensely attractive and powerful and must cause people to ask, 'How can these people live like this?'

Reflection

Read Psalm 96.

This psalm shows how extensive God's plan is and how we need to open our mouths to sing, praise, declare, worship and say how great our God is. It also highlights how he is to be the object not just of our praise but also of the praise of all nations. In fact, the earth itself is to praise its Maker, creation joining with us in a song of praise (verses 11–13).

1 The psalm tells us that however much praise is lifted to the Lord, it is no more than is 'due to his name' (verse 8).
2 So many of us (and I include myself here) are quiet about our faith, rather than upfront about it. It sometimes seems as if our beliefs and convictions have to be torn from us. But how can we stay silent, when we look at what we've studied so far and count all the reasons that we have to be grateful to God? How can we say nothing, when we remember that we haven't scratched the surface of all for which we should thank him? We are called to 'proclaim his salvation day after day' (verse 2).
3 Notice that we should be expressing our praise 'to the LORD' (verses 1–2) and displaying it to the peoples and nations (verse 3).
4 List all the reasons this psalm gives for the praising the Lord.

11

Gratitude and lament

How long, LORD? Will you forget me for ever?
(Psalm 13:1)

I wondered just how long they could maintain those smiles!

Many years ago, I was invited to speak to a small, recently planted church in northern England. When I arrived, I was met at the door by a couple who appeared to have identical smiles. A bit strange, I thought, but even stranger when I went inside to find that the whole congregation was trying to retain similarly beatific smiles. It got a bit ridiculous when the lady playing the flute in the worship band attempted to keep smiling as she played!

Please don't be under the impression that this book is saying that cultivating a habit of thankfulness will always make life good and will always give you a reason to smile. The promoters of prosperity theology today present them-selves as completely in control. All is well in their world; all is well between them and God. They have no questions, doubts or fears. How different from the great saints of the Bible. I wonder what the prosperity merchants make of the apostle Paul saying, 'I came to you in weakness with great fear and trembling' (1 Corinthians 2:3). There is a danger of failing to be real about our struggles and true feelings. The view that the Christian life is supposed to be a completely victorious one compounds the problem because we add guilt to our list of struggles. If we are not careful, we live life denying our feelings.

I hope that you are enjoying the brief psalm reflections. There are different kinds of psalm: those encompassing praise, wisdom and thanksgiving. But more than 50 of the 150 psalms are known as 'psalms of lament'. These are psalms in which the writer expresses deep sorrow or anger, or questions the state of a nation or his own experience, some of which we've already seen. The psalms are often expressions of raw emotion (see Psalm 88). Whole books of the Bible are given over to lament: Job, Lamentations and Habakkuk.

What do we learn from the fact that more than a third of the psalms are psalms of lament? Surely it underlines once more for us that, as Christians living in a fallen world, we are in a battle. If we're expecting a life that is all smiles, we are going to be very disappointed – even disillusioned. I have found Walter Brueggemann's categorization of the psalms very helpful. He recognizes psalms of orientation, disorientation and new orientation. Sometimes all three categories are seen in one psalm.[1]

For many of us, there are times in our Christian experience when all appears to be well and everything makes sense – these are times of orientation. But they don't last for ever, for we regularly experience times of disorientation when our world, or the world around us, seems to have gone mad. Nothing seems to make sense any more and, after crying out to God for help, it appears that we are met by silence.

Meet Habakkuk

How long, O LORD, must I call for help,
   but you do not listen?

Or cry out to you, 'Violence!'
  but you do not save?
(Habakkuk 1:2)

Here is a prophet, a man of God, in utter confusion. He looks around his world and he does not understand what God is doing or what he is not doing. Take a few moments to read the three chapters of Habakkuk and you will see that the prophecy ends with joy and assurance. Brueggemann suggests that this is the normal direction of travel for the believer. The period of disorientation may be hard, and sometimes long, but if, like Habakkuk, we hold on to God, bringing our confusion and questions to him, eventually a period of new orientation follows. We appreciate that God has been there throughout, seemingly silent but ever-present, and it is he who has brought us out of the pit and into the light once again.[2]

We need to seek to develop a habit of thanksgiving often in the middle of pain and confusion. Often, it is an act of faith to do so. It is one thing to develop this habit when all is going well in our lives, but quite another when everything appears to be collapsing around us. Habakkuk is a great example. If you read through the book, you will see that, towards the end, Habakkuk is contemplating utter disaster. In the final chapter, he might be describing the ultimate day of the Lord or the Babylonian invasion (described in Habakkuk 1); whichever way, the questions and concerns remain. But his response is a huge one of faith:

I heard and my heart pounded,
  my lips quivered at the sound;

113

decay crept into my bones,
  and my legs trembled.
Yet I will wait patiently for the day of calamity
  to come on the nation invading us.
Though the fig-tree does not bud
  and there are no grapes on the vines,
though the olive crop fails
  and the fields produce no food,
though there are no sheep in the sheepfold
  and no cattle in the stalls,
yet I will rejoice in the LORD,
  I will be joyful in God my Saviour.
(Habakkuk 3:16–18)

This is Habakkuk developing a habit of praise and thanks, even in the most extreme circumstances: 'yet I will rejoice *in the* LORD, I will be joyful *in God my Saviour*' (my emphasis). God remains unchanged; his salvation is as secure as ever.

> *'A great secret for us when times are hard*
> *is the patient waiting, the quiet trust*
> *and the long look.'*

A great secret for Habakkuk, and a great secret for us when times are hard, is the patient waiting, the quiet trust and the long look. Habakkuk knows now that the judgment of his people through the invasion of the Babylonians is inevitable. But he also knows that it will not be the end of the story. He knows the promises of God, he remembers the covenant and, although the fulfilment of those promises seems impossible when he writes, he knows his God and trusts his faithfulness.

He looks forward not just to a day when Israel will be judged but also to when her enemies will be judged: 'Yet I will wait patiently for the day of calamity to come on the nation invading us' (verse 16).

Cultivating a habit of praise is a huge part of the journey of faith. Enjoy those periods of orientation but realize that, in a fallen world, where we are the targets of a determined foe, they will not be your continual experience. Remember that for faith to grow and be strengthened, it must be tested; inevitably, those testing times will come.

Smiles may well be beyond you; if so, hang on to your experience of God, the biblical revelation of God and the certainty of his Word.

Reflection

Read Psalm 13.

1 God wants a real relationship with us. He wants to hear how we feel. What do you think about talking to God using language like the psalmist's?
2 Although we don't know the dilemma the psalmist was in when he wrote these words, it is clear that he is far from having all the answers. He refuses to remain silent. Have you learned to talk to God in the midst of confusion?
3 Although the psalmist's questions are many and his emotions raw, the last two verses of the psalm reveal his absolute determination to continue to trust in the Lord. His memory of the Lord's past goodness has been crucial: he says, 'for he has been good to me' (verse 6).

12

Radical gratitude in action

He will be with us throughout the journey until he takes us home.[1]

'We can never be accurate, Mr Maiden. But, without treatment, we think you have six to eight weeks to live. With treatment, possibly a year or longer.'

This news was imparted to me by my oncologist. For everyone, cancer is a personal journey; people react differently to treatment or to no treatment at all. It seemed as difficult for the oncologist to give Win, Hannah (our daughter-in-law) and me the news, poor chap, as it was for us to receive it. I was part of the way through writing this book when the bombshell hit. (In fact, my publisher changed the book title, inserting the word 'radical' to reflect my new situation.) But how could this be? In ten weeks, I'd gone from running up mountains to struggling just to get upstairs.

Win, as you can imagine, was distraught. While I went off for blood tests, she sobbed outside the Oncology Department and then forlornly stared at a stone wall. Fortunately, although Hannah was also upset, they were able to support each other. After the blood tests, I returned to Win and Hannah. Then someone said that I needed an X-ray immediately, so we walked to the relevant department. By now, I was feeling desperately ill. Of course, I had never died before but I honestly thought that this might well be the end. 'Give thanks in all circumstances,' I remembered amid my swirling thoughts and the crisp efficiency of the hospital staff.

For the first time in my life, I requested a wheelchair to return to the oncologist. On the way, I knew I was going to throw up violently and I was relieved to find a hospital toilet just in time. The oncologist informed us that I had to be promptly admitted to hospital. Frankly, they could have done what they liked with me at that moment – I was beyond caring.

The medical staff expected to discover a partial blockage of the bowel, but they didn't. After three days, I was discharged following some first-class medical care. I was well for the rest of the week, but then I began to deteriorate and I was rushed back into hospital. As before, the doctors expected to find a blockage and I spent another three days there. Once again, the problem settled down without any intervention; there was no blockage. 'Give thanks,' I thought, 'in all circumstances!'

I now had to face the diagnosis and big decisions. Although our children (Rebecca, Tim and Daniel) were adamant that Win and I had to decide, we very much wanted their input. An emotional family discussion followed. We came to the joint conclusion that if we did not give the life-prolonging treatment a try, we might regret it; my already shortened life would be shorter still.

And so, as I write, dear reader, the long, painful chemo-therapy journey has begun. I am one and a half weeks into a twelve-week course of treatment.

Thank you, Lord!

How do you give thanks in circumstances such as these? Is there any reason at all to say 'thank you' to God at such times?

When Jesus arrived at the grave of Lazarus, his friend had already been dead for four days. Witnessing the tears of Mary and the crowd who were with her, 'he was deeply moved in spirit and troubled' (John 11:33). The verb used here certainly seems to imply anger. Don Carson suggests this translation: 'He was outraged in spirit.'[2] Eugene Peterson paraphrases it thus: 'When Jesus saw her sobbing, a deep anger welled up within him' (*The Message*).

Feeling the absence of his friend, and looking at this scene of loss and Lazarus' weeping, broken sisters, Jesus is deeply moved not only by grief but also by anger. He is angry about the devastation that sin has caused in God's beautiful creation, especially by the wages of human sin – death. But, remarkably, in the middle of all of this, the words 'thank you' are on Jesus' lips. He approaches the tomb, orders that the stone guarding its entrance be taken away and prays, 'Father, I thank you that you have heard me' (verse 41). Quite clearly, in this horrific situation, he sees an opportunity for his Father to be glorified and for more to believe that he, Jesus, is the One sent from the Father – the Saviour (verse 42).

This has been my experience too. In the very darkest moments, to my total surprise, I have found myself uttering, 'Thank you, Lord. Thank you, Lord, that you are with me in this and that you will never leave me or forsake me.'

At a time when the children of Israel were feeling at their most vulnerable, God made a wonderful promise that cheered his people. It is a promise that has certainly been an encouragement to me recently. The people were coming to the end of their Babylonian exile, the length of which they knew (see Jeremiah 25:11). Their growing excitement must have been almost uncontainable as they thought of their feet again treading the Promised Land and walking the streets of the sacred city of Jerusalem. But, for many, it had become comfortable in Babylon. They had learnt their way around and learnt to cope with being in exile. For many, it seemed to be a little too much to replace the certainties of their Babylonian life, which had been their experience for seventy years, with stepping out with God into something that looked far less certain. And what about the sin that had resulted in their exile?

> Was it not the Lord,
>   against whom we have sinned?
> For they would not follow his ways;
>   they did not obey his law.
> So he poured out on them his burning anger,
>   the violence of war.
> It enveloped them in flames, yet they did not
>   understand;
>   it consumed them, but they did not take
>   it to heart.
> (Isaiah 42:24–25)

But there was also the glorious promise: 'When you walk through the fire, you will not be burned; the flames will not set you ablaze' (Isaiah 43:2–3). God's covenant love for his people was unchanging: he was going to redeem them and show them his personal love and care by summoning them by name (verse 1).

> *'God's covenant love for his people*
> *was unchanging.'*

122

This is 100 per cent true in my experience – the sense and evidence of God's presence has been so real. I am sure the Lord, in his goodness, gives an even more tangible sense of his presence at times of crisis. It's certainly one of the reasons why I have been able to give thanks in circumstances that have hit me and my family with such devastating force.

Thankful *for,* as well as in, all circumstances?

In recent days, I have been thinking a lot that there are reasons to give thanks to God *for* all circumstances, not just *in* all circumstances, however dreadful. There have been opportunities to grasp and lessons to learn – only because of this despicable cancer. Of course, I totally reject the Stoic idea that everything that happens in the universe is supposed to happen, so we should resign ourselves to our circumstances. I would never suggest for a moment that God chose me to get this disease and not Win. But because I have it, unique opportunities have come my way and, in this sense, I can be grateful for, as well as in, my present situation. It is at these times that, to my great surprise, I have found myself whispering, 'Thank you, Lord.'

Glory can be brought to our God, fresh opportunities can arise to testify to his grace and power, and lessons can be learned that never before have I been so driven to understand so deeply. I now enjoy days that I have only dreamt of for years. Let me explain.

While I'm lying in my hospital bed, the cleaner comes in to clean my room. For the next forty-five minutes, she sits on the windowsill and we talk 'Jesus' together. A Jewish woman comes to the ward to offer a hand massage. Now, I have never had a hand massage or even wanted to have a hand massage, but forty-five minutes of chatting about the Messiah are not to be missed! A Buddhist lady, with whom I have often wanted opportunities to share about Jesus, is now ready to talk about life after death. And I could go on.

Yes, it is a very strange season of life. I would never choose these circumstances and I do not believe that God chose them for me, but I live in a fallen world, a fallen creation, and God never promised me immunity from its consequences. But he did promise to be with me and those I love through it all. Even at the very lowest points, if I keep my eyes open, I see opportunities I have never had before.

A most remarkable woman who experienced this was the late Dr Helen Roseveare. Helen was working in what is now the Democratic Republic of Congo as a medical missionary. She was caught up in what became known as the Congo Crisis: five years of sustained brutality (1960–1965). By 1964, the Simba Rebellion (1963–1965), part of the Congo Crisis, brought real danger to Helen and several of her co-workers. Rebel soldiers carried out unspeakable acts. Helen and several of her colleagues were placed under arrest for five months. Helen's sufferings included the horror and torment of rape. Through the long dark nights, she sensed the Lord saying, 'These are not your sufferings. They're Mine. All I ask of you is the loan of your body.' She wrote later of her 'overwhelming sense of privilege, that Almighty God would stoop to ask of me, a mere nobody in a forest clearing in the jungles of Africa, something He needed'.[3] Incredibly, even in the appalling violence and horror, Helen found something to give to God to glorify him; in a far, far less horrific situation, that is what I am finding too.

Sorted?

Do I sound as though I have got everything together, that I have no questions or doubts? I hope not. The questions still come thick and fast. In recent years, after an extremely demanding life in Christian ministry, I have finally been able to give more time to Win and the family, which, it appears, is now being torn from me. I confess that the 'why' question begins to creep back in, proving that, for me at least, that sense of entitlement is one with which I still have to battle.

I love life: it is a joy. It is such a thrilling adventure to follow Jesus. You certainly don't know what the next day or, indeed, the next hour is going to bring. It's hard to grasp that the best is yet to come. I believe it and I preach it with conviction, but it remains hard to visualize it. So I am peaceful, trusting in the Lord, but sad as I think of the things that I will miss. I feel sadder for Win and the family than for me, but – here's the important bit – I'm 100 per cent secure. I'm secure in God, in his covenant faithfulness, in his sovereign grace and in his omnipotent power. The security is not in me or my faithfulness but in his. Indeed, his faithfulness is my only hope to keep me faithful to the end.

'I'm secure in God, in his covenant faithfulness, in his sovereign grace and in his omnipotent power.'

Before I go

Therefore, the kingdom of heaven is like a king who wanted to settle accounts with his servants. As he began the settlement, a man who owed him ten thousand bags of gold was brought to him. Since he was not able to pay, the master ordered that he and his wife and his children and all that he had be sold to repay the debt.

At this the servant fell on his knees before him. 'Be patient with me,' he begged, 'and I will pay back everything.' The servant's master took pity on him, cancelled the debt and let him go.
(Matthew 18:23–27)

With the unbelievable optimism of so many debtors, this servant falls at his master's feet, promising to pay back everything. Remarkably, the master takes pity on him, cancels the debt and lets him go.

This book is all about gratitude, but it is also all about grace. The story from Matthew 18 exemplifies grace: what this master did for his servant was totally undeserved. If the servant had lived and worked six days a week until the present day, he still would not have repaid his debt. The master was outrageously generous. But does the servant's experience of such extraordinary grace lead him to a life of gratitude and generosity? No, the very opposite. He is portrayed by Jesus as harsh and utterly cruel. He has not understood what he's received (see verses 28–30). After all these years of walking with Jesus, I still find myself from time to time behaving like this unmerciful servant.

Through the finished work of Christ, the slate was cleaned. It was grace – amazing grace, as John Newton would write and the church would sing. If we do not respond with grateful generosity to the grace we have received, it is because we have not understood the meaning of the cross. And the cross is the clearest, most powerful expression of divine grace. Is this not at the core of the Christian life when you drill right down? We are those who know the grace of God:

For it is by grace you have been saved, through faith – and this is not from yourselves, it is the gift of God – not by works, so that no one can boast.
(Ephesians 2:8–9)

For the grace of God has appeared that offers salvation to all people. It teaches us to say 'No' to ungodliness and worldly passions, and to live self-controlled, upright and godly lives in this present age, while we wait for the blessed hope – the appearing of the glory of our great God and Saviour, Jesus Christ, who gave himself for us to redeem us from all wickedness and to purify for himself a people that are his very own, eager to do what is good.
(Titus 2:11–14)

Trace our security, our forgiveness, our assurance and our hope back to its source, and we discover that it flows from the river of God's grace. We are nothing without grace. Because we have received, and daily continue to receive, such grace, our only response can be to become gracious, generous people ourselves. If we don't, then we have no understanding of all that we have received or of the immense price that has been paid to allow us to stand in grace today.

We who recognize how much we have received will freely give, counting it a privilege to do so. We will join the ranks of the cheerful givers Paul refers to in 2 Corinthians 9:7. We will be generous in every aspect of our lives: the giving of our time, our money and our eagerness to forgive when wronged.

Gratitude, generosity, grace

The subtitle of this book is *Recalibrating your heart in an age of entitlement*. To understand that being grateful is an issue of the mind and heart is crucially important. You will know by now that gratitude doesn't just happen on an impulse or whim – it's proactive and intentional.

I have a close friend who, at the end of every day, stops to recall and write down three specific occurrences for which she can thank God. She has found that there is repetition from one day to another, but that is not a problem; we all know that God proves his faithfulness repeatedly. She now has well over a thousand 'thank you' notes to turn to. Particularly when times are rough, it reassures her to turn to these notes and remind herself of the continual goodness of God.

It's a great exercise, but intentional gratitude must involve more than ticking boxes. We are crying out to God for heart change, to get to the place where we realize, as the apostle Paul did, that 'in me (that is, in my flesh) dwelleth no good thing' (Romans 7:18, KJV). We have nothing to offer to God but our sins and, as we have seen, it's there that the great exchange takes place. He offers us the righteousness of his Son in exchange for our sin and failure. Life then moves forwards; the full movement – from entitlement to grace, from demand to gratitude – will take the rest of our lives, and what a change it is!

My final word in a book on radical gratitude? Rely solely on the amazing grace of God.

Reflection

Read Psalm 46.

The diagnosis that I received while writing this book came out of a clear blue sky. One month, I was running up mountains; the next, I couldn't climb the stairs at home. You too must have had those startling, unforgettable occasions when you knew, from that moment onwards, life would never be the same again.

1 This psalm speaks of tumultuous times: 'Nations are in uproar, kingdoms fall' (verse 6). It seems as if the earth is giving way, as the mountains, which are a symbol of stability, are falling 'into the heart of the sea' (verse 2).

2 Yet, in the most extreme times, believers have an utterly secure refuge, 'an ever-present help in trouble' (verse 1). Even in trouble, they can know the joy and provision of the Lord (verses 5 and 7).

3 And they know that their present troubles are not the final story. The future is certain and very different (verses 8–9).

4 So we can 'be still, and know that [he is] God' (verse 10). He will be exalted among the nations and he is with us: 'the God of Jacob is our fortress' (verse 7).

Notes

Foreword

1 George Verwer, *Messiology: The mystery of how God works even when it doesn't make sense to us* (Farnham: CWR, 2015).

Introduction: thirty-six hours

1 <www.uk.om.org>
2 From a personal letter to a colleague; reproduced here with permission.
3 *Discipleship Matters: Dying to live for Christ* (Nottingham: IVP, 2015).

1 'You owe me'

1 <https://en.wikipedia.org/wiki/Entitlement>.
2 From the marketing description for Jean M. Twenge and W. Keith Campbell, *The Narcissism Epidemic: Living in an age of entitlement* (New York: Simon & Schuster, 2010); see <www.christianbook.com/narcissism-epidemic-living-the-age-entitlement/jean-twenge/9781416575993/pd/575993>, last accessed 4 February 2020.
3 John Gill, 'Students' Sense of Entitlement Angers Academics', *Times Higher Education Supplement*, 26, February 2009, p. 1.
4 Tony Walters, *Need: The New Religion – Exposing the language of need* (Nottingham: IVP, 2009).
5 Richard A. Easterlin, 'Will Raising the Incomes of All Increase the Happiness of All?', *Journal of Economic Behavior and Organization*, vol. 27 (1995), pp. 35–47; extracts taken from pp. 35 and 37–38.

6 Kenneth Copeland, *The Laws of Prosperity* (Shippensburg, Penn.: Destiny Image Publishers, May 2012), p. 51.

7 Augustine, *Confessions*, 1.1.1.

2 Blessed

1 Max Lucado, *Anxious for Nothing: Finding calm in a chaotic world* (Nashville, Tenn.: Thomas Nelson, 2017), p. 94.

2 John Stott, *The Message of Galatians*, The Bible Speaks Today (Leicester: IVP, 1993), p. 33.

3 A debtor

1 Jerry Bridges, *The Practice of Godliness* (Colorado Springs, Colo.: NavPress, 2016), p. 97.

2 Peter Maiden, *Discipleship Matters: Dying to live for Christ* (Nottingham: IVP, 2015), p. 100.

3 Quoted by Glynn Harrison in 'Why Gratitude Is Good for You', *Triple Helix* (Summer 2017); see <https://admin.cmf.org.uk/pdf/helix/summer17/gratitude.pdf>, last accessed 5 February 2020.

4 John Piper, *Don't Waste Your Life* (Leicester: IVP, 2005).

4 Ingratitude but choosing gratitude

1 Albert Barnes, *Notes, Explanatory and Practical, on the Epistles of Paul to the Ephesians, Philippians, and Colossians* (New York: Harper & Brothers, 1846), p. 248.

2 Martin Luther, *Lectures on Romans* (Louisville, Ky.: Westminster John Knox Press), 1961, p. 25.

3 <https://albertmohler.com/2016/11/23/thanksgiving-theological-act-mean-give-thanks>, last accessed 5 February 2020.

5 Disciplined gratitude, not grudging submission

1 Paul David Tripp, *New Morning Mercies: A gospel devotional* (Nottingham: IVP, 2014), p. 6.

2 Charles H. Spurgeon, *Psalms: Volume 1*, The Crossway Classic Commentaries (Leicester: IVP, 1994), p. 91.

6 Time out to remember

1 Nancy Leigh DeMoss, *Choosing Gratitude: Your journey to joy* (Chicago, Ill.: Moody Publishers, 2009), p. 63.

2 <www.abrahamlincolnonline.org/lincoln/speeches/fast.htm>, last accessed 6 February 2020.

7 Gratitude, success and riches: the good, the bad and the ugly

1 Glynn Harrison, 'Why Gratitude Is Good for You', *Triple Helix* (Summer 2017); see <https://admin.cmf.org.uk/ pdf/helix/summer17/gratitude.pdf>, last accessed 5 February 2020.

2 Jonathan Edwards, Part 3, *The Religious Affections*, <http:// leaderu.com/cyber/bookms/religaffect/rapt3sec02.html>, last accessed 18 February 2020.

3 Edwards, Part 3, *The Religious Affections*.

4 Edwards, Part 3, *The Religious Affections*.

5 John Piper, *A Godward Life: Savoring the supremacy of God in all life* (Sisters, Oreg.: Multnomah, 1997), pp. 213–214.

6 C. S. Lewis, *Mere Christianity* (Glasgow: Collins, 1990), p. 109. *Mere Christianity* by C. S. Lewis © copyright C. S. Lewis Pte Ltd 1942, 1943, 1944, 1952.

7 Quoted in Harold E. Will, *Will's Commentary on the New Testament: Volume 7 – I–II Corinthians*, 1995, p. 53.

8 Gratitude and sovereignty

1 Paul David Tripp, *New Morning Mercies: A gospel devotional* (Nottingham: IVP, 2014), p. 75.

9 Learning and contentment

1 Attributed to Benjamin Franklin.

2 Arthur M. Schlesinger, Jr, *The Cycles of American History* (Boston, Mass.: Houghton Mifflin, 1999), p. 27.

3 Rodney Clapp, 'Why the Devil Takes Visa: A response to the triumph of consumerism', *Christianity Today* (7 October 1996); see <https://christianitytoday.com/ct/1996/october7/6tb018.html>, last accessed 10 February 2020.

10 Gratitude as a weapon: fighting back in weakness

1 John Stott, *The Message of Acts*, The Bible Speaks Today (Leicester: IVP, 1991), p. 264.

2 'A little bird I am', in *Hymns of Worship and Remembrance* (Dubuque, Iowa: ECS Ministries, 2016).

11 Gratitude and lament

1 See Walter Brueggemann, *Spirituality of the Psalms* (Minneapolis, Minn.: Fortress Press, 2002).

2 Michael Wilcox, *The Message of Psalms 73 – 150: Songs for the people of God* (Nottingham: IVP, 2001), p. 22, discussing Walter Brueggemann's *The Psalms and the Life of Faith*, ed. Patrick D. Miller (Minneapolis, Minn.: Fortress Press, 1995).

12 Radical gratitude in action

1 Peter Maiden, *Discipleship Matters: Dying to live for Christ* (Nottingham: IVP, 2015), p. 157.

2 D. A. Carson, 'Jesus Outraged and Grief-Stricken', <https://
thevalueofsparrows.com/2017/01/31/jesus-jesus-outraged-and-
grief-stricken-by-d-a-carson>; cached at <https://cc.bingj.com/
cache.aspx?q=Carson+he+was+outraged+in+spirit&d=
4826053010981803&mkt=en-GB&setlang=en-GB&w=
A9I4kYQSshqSoobPk7xKLMLbIrWV7Od2>, last accessed
18 February 2020.
3 Justin Taylor, 'A Woman of Whom the World Was Not Worthy'
(7 December 2016), <www.thegospelcoalition.org/blogs/
justin-taylor/a-woman-of-whom-the-world-was-not-worthy-
helen-roseveare-1925-2016>, last accessed 10 February 2020.

Keswick Ministries

Our purpose

Keswick Ministries exists to inspire and equip Christians to love and live for Christ in his world.

God's purpose is to bring his blessing to all the nations of the world (Genesis 12:3). That promise of blessing, which touches every aspect of human life, is ultimately fulfilled through the life, death, resurrection, ascension and future return of Christ. All of the people of God are called to participate in his missionary purposes, wherever he may place them. The central vision of Keswick Ministries is to see the people of God equipped, inspired and refreshed to fulfil that calling, directed and guided by God's Word in the power of his Spirit, for the glory of his Son.

Our priorities

There are three fundamental priorities which shape all that we do as we look to serve the local church.

- *Hearing God's Word*: the Scriptures are the foundation for the church's life, growth and mission, and Keswick Ministries is committed to preach and teach God's Word in a way that is faithful to Scripture and relevant to Christians of all ages and backgrounds.
- *Becoming like God's Son*: from its earliest days, the Keswick movement has encouraged Christians to live godly lives in the power of the Spirit, to grow in Christlikeness and to live under his lordship in every area of life. This is God's will for his people in every culture and generation.
- *Serving God's mission*: the authentic response to God's Word is obedience to his mission, and the inevitable result of Christlikeness is sacrificial service. Keswick Ministries seeks to encourage committed discipleship in family life, work and society, and energetic engagement in the cause of world mission.

Our ministry

- *Keswick Convention.* The Convention attracts some 12,000 to 15,000 Christians from the UK and around the world to Keswick every summer. It provides Bible teaching for all ages, vibrant worship, a sense of unity across generations and denominations, and an inspirational call to serve Christ in the world. It caters for children of all ages and has

136

a strong youth and young adult programme. And it all takes place in the beautiful Lake District – a perfect setting for rest, recreation and refreshment.

- **Keswick fellowship.** For more than 140 years, the work of Keswick has had an impact on churches worldwide, not just through individuals being changed but also through Bible conventions that originate or draw their inspiration from the Keswick Convention. Today, there is a network of events that shares Keswick Ministries' priorities across the UK and in many parts of Europe, Asia, North America, Australia, Africa and the Caribbean. Keswick Ministries is committed to strengthening the network in the UK and beyond, through prayer, news and cooperative activity.
- **Keswick teaching and training.** Keswick Ministries is developing a range of inspiring, equipping, Bible-centred teaching and training that focuses on 'whole-of- life' discipleship. This builds on the same concern that started the Convention: that all Christians live godly lives in the power of the Spirit in all spheres of life in God's world. Some of the events focus on equipping. They are smaller and more intensive. Others focus on inspiring. Some are for pastors, others for those in other forms of church leadership, while many are for any Christian. All courses aim to see participants return home refreshed to serve.
- **Keswick resources.** Keswick Ministries produces a range of books, devotionals and study guides as well as digital resources to inspire and equip Christians to live for Christ. The printed resources focus on the core foundations of Christian life and mission and help Christians in their walk with Christ. The digital resources make teaching and sung worship from the Keswick Convention available in a variety of ways.

Our unity

The Keswick movement worldwide has adopted a key Pauline statement to describe its gospel inclusivity: 'all one in Christ Jesus' (Galatians 3:28). Keswick Ministries works with evangelicals from a wide variety of church backgrounds, on the understanding that they share a commitment to the essential truths of the Christian faith as set out in our statement of belief.

Our contact details

T: 01768 780075
E: info@keswickministries.org
W: www.keswickministries.org
Mail: Keswick Ministries, Rawnsley Centre, Main Street, Keswick, Cumbria, CA12 5NP, England

Discipleship Matters

Peter Maiden

ISBN: 978 1 78359 355 2
176 pages paperback

Discipleship involves a gentle journey with our Saviour. Its demands will dovetail happily with our carefully crafted plans.

Wrong. Peter Maiden pulls no punches as he looks at what a disciple should look like today. Are we prepared to follow Jesus' example? Lose our lives for his sake? Live counterculturally in a world that values power, prestige and money, and constantly puts self at the centre?

Of all people, Jesus, the Son of God, has the authority to require this of us. And he's calling us to a relationship, not to a set of rules or a miserable, spartan existence. In fact, it is through losing our lives that we find them, and thereby discover the source of pure joy.

What a pity we set the bar too low.